Emerging identities in virtual exchange

Written by Francesca Helm

R research-publishing.net

Research-publishing.net

Published by Research-publishing.net, a not-for-profit association
Voillans, France, info@research-publishing.net

Emerging identities in virtual exchange
Written by Francesca Helm

Typeset by Research-publishing.net
Cover design by © Raphaël Savina (raphael@savina.net)

ISBN13: 978-2-490057-19-1 (Ebook, PDF, colour)
ISBN13: 978-2-490057-20-7 (Ebook, EPUB, colour)
ISBN13: 978-2-490057-18-4 (Paperback - Print on demand, black and white)
Print on demand technology is a high-quality, innovative and ecological printing method; with which the book is never 'out of stock' or 'out of print'.

British Library Cataloguing-in-Publication Data.
A cataloguing record for this book is available from the British Library.

Legal deposit, UK: British Library.
Legal deposit, France: Bibliothèque Nationale de France - Dépôt légal: juillet 2018.

Table of contents

Acknowledgements

There are many people to whom I am indebted for making this book possible. First of all to Melinda Dooly, my PhD supervisor, mentor, and friend, for your guidance in leading me through this journey, and for your patience. *Moltes gràcies* to the GREIP[1] research group at Universitat Autònoma de Barcelona for the lively, plurilingual workshops, data sessions, dialogic spaces, and *tribunal de la seguiment de tesis*. Thanks also to Nicolas Guichon, Shannon Sauro, and Laia Canals for the stimulating discussion and feedback received at the *defensa de la tesi*. A special thanks to Steve Thorne and Katja Riikonen for taking the time to review chapters of the draft version of this book and make valuable suggestions to improve them.

I would also like to thank the Soliya community with whom I have engaged virtually since 2008 in various guises, in particular to Waidehi Gokhale and Salma Elbeblawi for encouraging and facilitating this research, for the many discussions we have had about virtual exchange, and for granting me permission to use the data. Thanks also to my co-facilitators, coaches, trainers, coordinators, and participants whose interactions and invaluable feedback have challenged my assumptions and led me on many a reflexive and exploratory journey.

Thanks to colleagues and friends from the University of Padova and from UNICollaboration from whom I have learnt so much through our projects and discussions, at conferences and online. There are too many to name everyone, but special thanks go to Sarah Guth for the many years of intense collaboration.

I would like to thank Sylvie Thouësny for reminding me that going open access was the ethical choice for publishing, and for all the support that she and her

---

1. http://grupsderecerca.uab.cat/greip/en

team have given me through the editorial process in getting this final version to press.

The publication of this book and making it open access was made possible by the Spanish Ministry of Economy, Industry & Competitivity: Proyectos I+D del Programa Estatal de Fomento de la Investigación Científica y Técnica de Excelencia. Konect project (Knowledge for Network-based Education, Cognition & Teaching[2]). Grant number: EDU2013-43932-P.

The author and publisher also wish to thank: Soliya for the permission to reproduce the images in this book for which they hold copyright; Springer Nature as parts of Chapter 1 have been adapted by permission from Springer Nature: Springer, *Critical approaches to online intercultural language education* by Helm, *F. in Language, education and technology. Encyclopedia of language and education* edited by S. L. Thorne and S. May, Copyright © 2017, Springer International Publishing AG (Helm, 2017); the publishers of the journal *Language Learning & Technology* as parts of the book were previously published in the article *Challenges in transcribing multimodal data: a case study* written by F. Helm and M. Dooly, Copyright © 2017, Francesca Helm & Melinda Dooly (Helm & Dooly, 2017).

All opinions, mistakes, and errors in this book are, of course, my own.

---

2. http://grupsderecerca.uab.cat/greip/en/content/knowledge-network-based-education-cognition-teaching-konect

Transcription conventions

The multimodal transcript is in tabular format in an attempt to show the synchronicity of the spoken and written modes. The transcript conventions have been adapted from those developed by Jefferson (1984).

(2s)	Number in brackets indicates a time gap in seconds.
(.) (..)	Pauses shorter than a second.
(( ))	A description enclosed in a double bracket indicates a non-speech sound.
-	A dash indicates the sharp cut-off of the prior sound or word.
lo:ng	Colons indicate that the speaker has stretched the preceding sound or letter.
(word)	The transcriber's guess at an unclear part of the recording.
( )	Unclear speech or noise to which no approximation is made.
.	A full stop indicates a stopping fall in tone. It does not necessarily indicate the end of a sentence.
?	A question mark indicates a rising inflection. It does not necessarily indicate a question.
Under	Underlined fragments indicate speaker emphasis.
CAPITALS	Words in capitals mark a section of speech noticeably louder.
° °	Degree signs are used to indicate that the talk they encompass is spoken noticeably quieter.
< slow > >fast<	'Less than' and 'More than' signs indicate that the talk they encompass was produced noticeably slower or faster.
[ ]	Square brackets indicate comments about visual mode.
'hh, hh	Speaker's in-breath and out-breath respectively.
Hehh, hahh	Laughter syllables with some attempt to capture 'colour'.
Wo(h)rd	Indicates laughter within words.

Foreword

There has been considerable talk about the future of research and practice in education. Occasionally the discourse tends to the euphoric, sometimes it strays more to the dystopic. Public debates often explore how educators can and should meet society's demands in the globalised, interconnected geopolitical situations of today. Voiced concern about learners (as future 'global', 'digitalised' citizens) regarding what skills and competencies they must have and what knowledge they are constructing (or not), both formally and informally, are prevalent in frequent public debates. However, no matter where one stands on the issues of debate, there is a general consensus that education will be transformed in the next decades in order to accommodate the rapid technological, socio political, geographical, and environmental changes the world is experiencing, not to mention the many changes on the human level that we all live on a daily basis.

Of course society – and subsequently education – have always undergone continual change. Nonetheless, the past decades have brought about an almost vertiginous sense of change. Twenty years ago, Appadurai (1996) described these changes in a model of 'transcultural flows' that theorise five different domains of transcultural movements: ethnoscapes (involving flow of people); mediascapes (flow of information); technoscapes (flow of technology); financescapes (flows of finance); and ideoscapes (flow of ideology or ideas). These changes have an impact on how the world is perceived: for millenniums social life was largely inertial; traditions marked and influenced learning and individuals perceived a relatively finite set of possibilities for their future.

Now education must find a way to encompass, address, and embrace all of these shifting 'scapes'. This can be disconcerting. As the online journal 'Education Week' has pointed out, "when it comes to predicting the future of work, top economists and technologists are all over the map". Faced with this uncertainty, teachers, administrators and policy makers inevitably feel consternation and anxiety. Educational research, carried out in conjunction with teachers and students, can provide key answers on how to shape the future of learning[1].

The KONECT project[2] (EDU2013-43932-P) set out to gather and analyse innovative approaches to education in primary and secondary education in several countries in order to draw up guidelines, teaching materials, and books that are based on transnational, technology-enhanced, multilingual, interdisciplinary and issue-based teaching and learning. This book in particular draws on a meticulous study based on a relatively recent pedagogical approach to teaching and learning (virtual interaction), providing key insight into the learning processes – and individual learner identities – that emerge from interaction in online environments.

The study discussed in this book shows how online learner identities are discursively constructed between the participants and that these identities are dynamic and fluid. The author carefully outlines how the actions of the 'teachers' (facilitators in this case), the online platform, and even the local environments of the participants can affect the outcomes, and identity construction of the participants, during dialogue-based learning sessions in an online environment. The arguments are laid out for a critical interrogation of the predominant discursive construction of telecollaborative participants' identities in static and essentialist terms – identities which are often 'marked' through a focus on national languages, identities, and cultures.

Given the importance of intercultural education in telecollaborative language learning, the relevance of this point should not be underestimated. Studies show that too often intercultural education falls into the concept of a fixed static entity (see Barbot & Dervin, 2011; Finch & Nynäs, 2011). This is compounded by the difficulties of actually defining intercultural competences and intercultural

1. Parts of this preface are already published in the introduction to teaching materials developed by the KONECT project; https://www.konectproject.com

2. This book has been supported through funding provided by the Spanish Ministry of Economy, Industry & Competitivity: Proyectos I+D del Programa Estatal de Fomento de la Investigación Científica y Técnica de Excelencia through the KONECT project. Grant number: EDU2013-43932-P); 2013-2017 (grant extended to March 2018); https://www.konectproject.com

awareness; as is witnessed by the many different terms that have been used to describe them: multi/pluriculturalism, intercultural sensitivity, global citizenship, just to name a few examples. These theoretical questions are exacerbated by ethical issues when teachers have to 'assess' gains in intercultural awareness (see Borghetti, 2011). It seems to be a 'Catch-22' of measuring 'internal' gains through 'external' traits and behaviours – all of which are contingent upon the context in which the individual is interacting. As Helm points out in this book, teachers are responsible for creating the situated contexts they ask their students to participant in – and this underscores the need to be more aware of their own ideological underpinnings which will influence the identities they (both teachers and students) make relevant.

In this sense, the contents of this book go far to critique and advance previous knowledge in an area that bridges technology with applied sciences of education, language learning, cultural mediation and intercultural communication. It also presents innovative and inspiring pedagogical recommendations for online dialogic learning that can provide a cornerstone for promoting critical and reflective intercultural transformative learning. This latter point underscores how opportune this book is, given the current geopolitical occurrences of global upheaval (unprecedented numbers of displaced persons, acts of terrorism, upswing of racism and nationalism in mainstream politics, etc.). This book serves as an excellent model for what politically-engaged pedagogy (and research) can be.

Dr Melinda Dooly
Universitat Autònoma de Barcelona

Introduction

This book, as the title suggests, is about exploring identities within an educational framework called *Virtual Exchange*. Some readers may not be familiar with this term, or indeed the practice of virtual exchange, so my first task in this introduction is to provide a definition, which is no easy task given the many types of virtual exchange currently in use.

In a recent project funded by the European Commission[1] which brought together practitioners, researchers, and virtual exchange providers, we set ourselves the task of coming up with a common definition that all partners felt comfortable with. What we came up with was by no means a slender definition, but rather a complex, articulated definition of virtual exchange which has provided this volume with a useful starting point.

> "Virtual exchange is a **practice**, supported by research, that consists of sustained, technology-enabled, people-to-people education programmes or activities in which constructive communication and interaction takes place between individuals or groups who are geographically separated and/or from different cultural backgrounds, with the support of educators or facilitators. Virtual exchange combines the deep impact of intercultural dialogue and exchange with the broad reach of digital technology.
>
> Virtual exchange aims to allow an increasing number of people to have a meaningful intercultural experience as part of their formal and/or non-formal education. This type of activity may be situated in educational programmes across the curriculum in order to increase

---

1. The EVOLVE (Evidence-Validated Online Learning through Virtual Exchange) project, launched in January 2018 and led by Sake Jager at the University of Groningen, aims to mainstream virtual exchange as an innovative form of collaborative international learning across disciplines in higher education institutions in Europe and beyond; https://evolve-erasmus.eu/

mutual understanding and global citizenship, as well as in non-formal education projects. Virtual exchange also fosters the development of what have been recognised as employability skills, such as digital competence (the ability to communicate and collaborate effectively online), foreign language competence, communication skills, media literacy, and the ability to work in a diverse cultural context.

Virtual exchange is:
- **sustained**: unfolding over time with regular, intensive interaction;
- **technology-enabled**: using new media, digital, and/or mobile technologies;
- **synchronous or near-synchronous**: based on regular meetings using high social presence media;
- **people-to-people**: involving inclusive, intercultural collaboration and dialogue that bridges differences and distances and inspires action with a long term positive impact on relationships;
- **learner-led**: following the philosophy of dialogue where participants are the main recipients and the main drivers of knowledge; learning through dialogue means that participants will be seeking mutual understanding and co-creating knowledge based on their own experiences.
- **facilitated**: with the support of trained facilitators and/or educators;
- **educational**: integrated into formal and/or non-formal educational programmes and activities to develop measurable increases in the skills, knowledge, and attitudes that foster pro-social behaviours;
- **structured** to foster mutual understanding: covering topics related to identity, empathy, perspective taking, critical reflection, intercultural understanding, and helping participants to engage in constructive conversations in the face of ontological and epistemological differences; a key tenet of virtual exchange is that intercultural understanding and awareness are not automatic outcomes of contact between different groups/cultures"[2].

---

2. https://evolve-erasmus.eu/about-evolve/what-is-virtual-exchange/

It is perhaps easier to define what virtual exchange does **not** represent. Learning approaches that do not align with what we have described as virtual exchange include distance learning courses, massive open online courses, and virtual mobility formats which do not include sustained interactions between small groups of students. In these aforementioned models of online education, the focus is very much on content rather than sustained interaction between students, and thus the virtual exchange mandate for intense person-to-person engagement is not met. In addition, social media groups, unmoderated and unstructured online interactions, and one-off video-conferences are not considered virtual exchange for they lack a pedagogy oriented towards sustained interpersonal interaction.

A possible reason why defining virtual exchange is challenging is that somewhat heterogeneous virtual exchange models and approaches have been developed, in various contexts, in order to meet a diverse range of objectives.

Language educators have for over two decades been practising and researching what we call *telecollaboration*, defined in 2003 by Julie Belz as "institutionalized, electronically mediated intercultural communication under the guidance of a languacultural expert (i.e. teacher) for the purposes of foreign language learning and the development of intercultural competence" (p. 2). This pedagogic practice has traditionally entailed class-to-class exchanges designed around activities collaboratively created by language teachers working in different contexts who share similar objectives of having students use language to engage with 'others' in authentic meaning-making[3]. Students interact with one another in various configurations, from one to one, small groups, or whole classes, using asynchronous and/or synchronous internet communication tools.

On the other hand organisations have developed and implement specific models of virtual exchange grounded in principles of inter-group theory, dialogue, and conflict transformation[4]. These are larger-scale exchanges involving hundreds

---

3. For an in depth historical overview of the pedagogical underpinnings of telecollaboration/virtual exchange, see the introductory chapter by Dooly and O'Dowd (2018) in the book entitled: *In this together: teachers' experiences with transnational, telecollaborative language learning projects.*

4. For example, Soliya (www.soliya.net) and the Sharing Perspectives Foundation (https://sharingperspectivesfoundation.com/)

of students from multiple institutions across the world and have been developed to engage students in small-group facilitated dialogue sessions in which they address socio-political issues such as immigration, European citizenship, politics, religion, and terrorism, to name but a few.

This book[5] attempts to bring together my experience in these two different areas of virtual exchange, though I am aware that virtual exchange has also developed in other contexts[6]. In it, I draw on my identities as a language teacher, practitioner, facilitator and researcher of both models of virtual exchange. Adopting an ethnographic, interaction-based approach, I analyse interactions from a group of students that took part in a large scale, online facilitated dialogue model of virtual exchange, the Soliya Connect Program. But first of all, some considerations as to why one would want to engage students in virtual exchange.

1.1.   Why virtual exchange?

Virtual exchange is not a goal in itself[7], and as it gradually becomes part of institutional practices and educational policy, it is important to ask ourselves what our aims are as we engage students in this activity. One possible reason might be to 'equip learners to participate together in a global world', but what exactly do we mean by this?

It is worth taking the time to examine some of the assumptions that underlie our practice and the beliefs we have about knowledge systems (epistemologies) in a changing world.

5. This book is based on my PhD thesis, "I'm not disagreeing, I'm just curious": Exploring identities through multimodal interaction in virtual exchange, which can be found at: https://www.educacion.gob.es/teseo/mostrarRef.do?ref=1351668

6. For example, the Collaborative Online International Learning (COIL) Centre of the State University of New York (SUNY) has developed a model of interdisciplinary class to class virtual exchange whose aim is to extend the benefits of international education to a broader range of students and staff of universities.

7. This alludes to 2011 discussions about internationalisation of higher education, when in face of the growing obsession with numbers and statistics regarding mobility and internationalisation, Brandenburg highlighted that internationalisation is not a goal in itself, but a means to an end, an instrument to achieve something; https://ejournals.bc.edu/ojs/index.php/ihe/article/view/8533/7667

Andreotti and de Souza (2008) offer a set of pedagogical tools, stimuli for reflection which can help us, as educators, engage with debates around the role of global learning/education in a 'knowledge society'. I have found these to be particularly useful in exploring the issues around why and how we might engage learners in virtual exchange. One of the tools presents us with two different ways of analysing this idea that the role of education is to 'equip learners to participate together in a global world', deconstructing the terms 'global society', 'participate' and 'equip' according to two dominant ways of thinking and of viewing the world.

The Newtonian, or Modernist way of thinking, is represented by the metaphor of the world as a mechanical clock, whereby a global society is structured and ordered. This type of world can be understood as a whole through the analysis of its parts and is thus predictable and can be engineered. A 'good and ideal society' is based on a universalist view of what is real and ideal, which determines a specific course of action to achieve this. Interpretations which diverge from the above assumptions are deemed not completely 'rational' or 'developed' and thus are suppressed or ignored.

Participation in a Modernist world would entail having absorbed the 'right' information and being able to reproduce, or adapt oneself to, authorised ways of thinking and behaving (similar to what Freire (1984) called the 'banking model' of education). Conflict and difference would be seen as obstacles to be suppressed, controlled, or managed, because establishing consensus is a priority. Equipping learners to participate in this kind of society would thus involve the transmission of specific knowledge and the nurturing of skills and mindsets which would support the maintenance and continuing realisation of this type of society (Andreotti & de Souza, 2008, p. 9).

An alternative way of viewing the world is based on a complex systems paradigm, using the metaphor of the world as a living system with inter-related parts and processes. From this perspective, global society is imagined as diverse, inter-connected, multi-faceted, and in constant flux. Transformations constantly take place as the different parts and systems interact with one another, but these systems cannot survive in isolation, so it is the exchanges and relations within and between systems which drive change. Different meanings and interpretations, ways of seeing and knowing, are seen as representing the diversity of this world, which is central to survival (Andreotti & de Souza, 2008, p. 10).

Within this world view, participation would mean the evaluation, interrogation, and connection of different types of information. This would entail being able to live with difference, insecurity, and viewing conflict as being potentially productive. Equipping learners for this type of world would mean exposing them to different models of thinking, strategies for establishing relationships, shifting positions and perspectives according to changing contexts, and being able to live with and navigate complexity and uncertainty.

Virtual exchange, as conceptualised in this volume, is more grounded in the second of the world views described above. It is seen as a reflective, experiential approach to education which aims to encourage participants to engage with difference, to assess and interrogate information and perspectives, and to explore and negotiate identities, their own as well as those of others, through online, intercultural interactions with distant peers.

1.2. A brief history of virtual exchange

Though the term *virtual exchange* is relatively new, the practice is not and has developed in several different spheres: intergroup dialogue and conflict transformation, global learning, and foreign language education – and quite possibly other fields that I am not aware of.

The origins of virtual exchange have been linked to the work of iEARN and the New York/Moscow Schools Telecommunications Project[8] (NYS-MSTP) which was launched in 1988 by Peter Copen and the Copen Family Fund.

---

8. https://en.wikipedia.org/wiki/User:Calfux/sandbox#cite_note-2

This project stemmed from a perceived need to connect youth from the two countries during a time which was marked by tensions between the United States and the U.S.S.R. that had developed during the Cold War. With the institutional support of the Academy of Sciences in Moscow, and the New York State Board of Education, a pilot programme between 12 schools in each nation, was established. Students worked in both English and Russian on projects based on their curricula, which had been designed by participating teachers. The programme expanded in the early 1990's to include China, Israel, Australia, Spain, Canada, Argentina, and the Netherlands. The early 1990's saw the establishment of the organisation iEARN[9] which became officially established in 1994 and included the countries which took part in this first project.

These "global learning networks" challenged the prevalent top-down, transmission model of education as they were based on online intercultural collaborations which derived their impact from "a vision of how education can enact, in microcosm, a radical restructuring of power relations both in domestic and global arenas" (Cummins & Sayers, 1995, p. 8). The approach which is embodied in these projects, such as the Orillas project, centered around collaborative critical inquiry in which students are encouraged to reflect critically on experiential and social issues.

In the field of foreign language education, virtual exchange is more commonly associated with telecollaboration (Belz, 2002; Dooly, 2008; Dooly & O'Dowd, 2018; Guth & Helm, 2010; O'Dowd, 2006; Warschauer, 1996) or online intercultural exchange[10] (O'Dowd, 2007; O'Dowd & Lewis, 2016). This practice developed around a critical perspective on the 'traditional' foreign language classroom, which was seen to offer learners limited opportunities for interaction and for learning. Like the iEARN projects, it has drawn inspiration from the work of educators such as Mario Lodi with his class newspapers in Italy, Celestine Freinet's work in France early in the 20th century, and from

---

9. http://www.iearn.org/

10. I shall use the terms *online intercultural exchange* and *telecollaboration* to refer to the literature about virtual exchange in foreign language educations to be consistent with the literature.

global education networks such as Riel's (1993) Learning Circles project which opened up opportunities for interactions outside the classroom (see Lewis & O'Dowd, 2016 for an overview of the history of online intercultural exchange, and Dooly & O'Dowd, 2018 for a history its pedagogical underpinnings).

1.3. Foreign language learning, research and virtual exchange

A considerable body of research has been carried out by foreign language educators and researchers of telecollaboration and online intercultural exchange, with hundreds of journal articles on the theme, dedicated volumes (Belz & Thorne, 2006; Dooly, 2008; Guth & Helm, 2010; O'Dowd, 2007; Warschauer & Kern, 2000), journal special editions (Belz, 2003; Lewis, Chanier, & Youngs, 2011), and a book series, *Telecollaboration in Education* (e.g. Dooly & O'Dowd, 2012). Telecollaboration research has progressed from collections of classroom practice and anecdotal research to in-depth studies of online interaction and exchange. Research studies have reported on the many outcomes of different telecollaborative projects, mainly in higher education contexts, such as increased motivation and linguistic output (Kern, Ware, & Warschauer, 2004; Warschauer, 1996, 1998), gains in language development, accuracy and fluency (Kötter, 2003; Lee, 2006), intercultural communicative competence (Belz, 2007; Möllering & Levy, 2012; O'Dowd, 2006), pragmatic competence (Belz & Kinginger, 2003), and multimodal communicative competence (Dooly & Hauck, 2012; Hampel & Hauck, 2006), to name but a few.

The research has also documented failure and difficulties, which have been attributed to a wide range of factors. The assumption that intercultural learning would automatically result from the contact and interaction with distant 'others' was challenged from the outset as researchers have, Lamy and Goodfellow (2010) point out, readily identified difficulties, tensions, and failure in telecollaboration projects (e.g. Kramsch & Thorne, 2002). There are some critical issues in telecollaboration and online intercultural exchange that are particularly relevant to this study on identity and virtual exchange. The first regards the way culture is sometimes conceptualised in telecollaborative exchanges and the limited identity positionings for learners which result from this (Helm, 2017). The second is the difficulty of engaging learners in online intercultural exchange, so that they go beyond 'assumptions' of similarity and adopt a critical, intercultural stance (Ware & Kramsch, 2005). I shall explore these a little further in the pages to follow.

1.3.1. Critical issue 1: limited identity positionings

Participants in telecollaborative exchanges tend to be discursively constructed in terms of national languages, identities, and cultures (Train, 2006) which are represented as static and essentialist, that is they are seen to have an underlying and unchanging 'essence'. As Train (2006) writes, the field is characterised by "the assumption of one-nation-one-culture-one-self as the only desirable model of community, language, culture and identity" (p. 257). This assumption is closely linked to 'native speaker' ideologies and 'standards' of national languages which are still dominant in the discourses of foreign language teaching and, indeed, online intercultural exchange. These ideologies have marginalised and limited the identity positioning of the language and intercultural learner.

Telles (2014), who has promoted and carried out extensive research on *Teletandem*[11], for example, has found that many of the interactions taking place between pairs of students are characterised by inherent essentialism. The content discussed in the interactions is, he writes, based on repetitive, common sense conceptualisations of nationality and culture, and partners focus on marking differences in the interactions. As Telles (2014) writes:

> "In line with Piller's thoughts, the discussions deal with the twin problems of essentialism ('people have a culture') and reification of national and ethnic identity as culture ('people from group X behave in ways that are static, internally similar and different from other groups') (Piller, 2012, pp. 6-7)" (p. 4).

---

11. Teletandem is a bilingual model of online intercultural exchange

This position has been echoed by several other researchers, for example Ortega and Zyzik (2008) who highlight the persistent identification of a fixed culture with "so-called native speakers as a homogeneous group" (p. 341). Part of the problem in their view is the non-questioning of the meaning of 'culture' in the models of intercultural competence (Kramsch, 2001) that telecollaboration practitioners have drawn upon (Helm, 2017, p. 6).

The potential of online intercultural exchange in offering opportunities for identity work has been recognised by scholars such as Block (2007/2014), Kramsch (2009), and Norton (2000/2013), but is yet to be fully and broadly achieved. As Norton and Toohey (2011) attest, most research on identity has been carried out in the field of second (L2) language learning and, in particular, immigrant learners (Pavlenko & Blackledge, 2004; Norton, 2000/2013). Identity performance in digital contexts such as social networks, online gaming sites, and fanfiction has recently become a rich area of research (Thorne, Sauro, & Smith, 2015), but much less work has been carried out in the foreign language classroom (Block, 2007/2014) or in the fields of online intercultural exchange and computer-assisted language learning (Gee & Lee, 2016).

At the *Second International Conference on Telecollaboration in Higher Education*[12], David Little (2016) pointed out that foreign language education is still characterised by a mismatch between aspirations and outcomes. He described a widespread failure to question traditional teaching and learning dynamics and to engage students' identities in the process of language learning. He also provocatively asked:

> "Will emerging telecollaborative practice contribute to the evolution of a new learning-and-teaching dynamic that extends learners' identity and their capacity for agentive behaviour, or will it simply add some extra limbs to a pedagogical tradition that has long been sclerotic?" (Little, 2016, p. 55).

---

12. http://www.ub.edu/realtic/en/second-international-conference-on-telecollaboration-in-higher-education-dublin-2016/

1.3.2. Critical issue 2: fostering a critical, intercultural stance in learners

The second issue which I address is perhaps the one that has led to the most persistent questioning and reflection: the difficulty in getting students to engage in deeper levels of interaction (Dooly, 2011; Helm, 2013, Kramsch & Thorne, 2002; O'Dowd, 2003; Ware & Kramsch, 2005) so that they move beyond the 'assumption of similarity' and manage to take a critical, intercultural stance (Ware, 2005; Ware & Kramsch, 2005).

In order to address this issue, we need to ask ourselves what it is we are aiming for in our practice. The communicative competence models on which much of foreign language teaching and also telecollaboration are based have been called into question by many (Kramsch, 2014; Lamy & Goodfellow, 2010; Little, 2016; Schneider & von der Emde, 2006; Train, 2006). As stated by Helm (2017), some of the sociocultural strategies embodied in this model, particularly those for avoiding conflict, and the notion of effective or successful communication are seen as representing a form of cultural imperialism.

Schneider and von der Emde (2006) take issue in particular with Savignon and Sysoyev's (2002) "sociocultural strategy for maintaining a dialogue of cultures", which is based on the assumption that "mutual understanding" will take place in a "spirit of peace" if one of the interlocutors suppresses their points of view. This "strategy", they point out, implicitly requires learners to "adopt questionable [native speaker] standards and forego their privileges as [non-native speakers]" (Schneider and von der Emde, 2006, p.181). The findings of other researchers, for example Ware in her 2005 study, support this stance as she found that in order to avert miscommunication, that is misunderstandings or tensions in communication with their peers, students used avoidance strategies which could lead to "missed" communication, that is to say, missed opportunities for meaningful intercultural learning (Ware, 2005, p. 66). This preoccupation with conflict avoidance evokes the Newtonian or Modernist view of the world described earlier in this chapter where global society is structured and ordered and where conflict and difference are seen as obstacles to be suppressed, controlled, or managed.

Drawing on the work of Bakhtin (1986) on dialogue and the conceptualisation of language as a site of struggle, Schneider and von der Emde (2006) argue that it is more important to help students feel comfortable with conflict than to encourage them to deny their own cultural approaches to disagreement or rush to find common ground, for almost inevitably it is the dominant culture which establishes what ground is common. They propose a dialogic approach as this type of approach posits conflict not only as an inherent feature of intercultural exchange, but also as a value. Dialogue allows for the existence of differences without trying to overcome or 'tame' them.

Schneider and von der Emde's (2006) conceptualisation of online intercultural education as a 'site for struggle' has much in common with Ortega and Zyzik's (2008) emphasis on the need to conceptualise computer mediated interactions as "complex and contested sites for intercultural negotiation and reconstruction" rather than as "inherently productive moments for bringing about intercultural understanding" (p. 338).

Here again, the literature on identity and language learning is potentially relevant, in particular the notion of investment which presupposes that as learners interact

> "they are not only exchanging information with target language speakers, but they are constantly organizing and reorganizing a sense of who they are and how they relate to the social world. Thus an investment in the target language is also an investment in a learner's own identity, an identity which is constantly changing across time and space" (Norton, 2000/2013, p. 51).

1.4. Why explore identity in virtual exchange?

Identity can be seen as a key construct to successful learning because it links the learner to the social world, both inside and outside of the classroom. By focussing on the fluidity and co-construction of identity in interactions, we can move away from static and monolithic representations of culture and essentialist understandings of the intercultural (Dervin, 2015). Identities can be empowering and disempowering, they can be assumed and they can be challenged. Opportunities for 'identity work' can be created by educators both within the classroom and also beyond. Through the use of online technologies for virtual exchange, students can be offered opportunities for identity construction and negotiation through authentic interaction with geographically distant peers.

This book is aimed at educators and graduate students interested in learning more about virtual exchange and exploring the kind of interactions that can take place in online facilitated dialogue. It is also of potential relevance to scholars of identity, intercultural learning, global education, foreign language teaching, and technology in education. It is based on a study which consisted in the development and application of a theoretical framework for the study of identity as it emerges in interaction in a specific virtual exchange context. The original study consisted in the transcription and micro-analytical analysis of the multimodal communication from three two-hour online dialogue sessions from one group of young people from Egypt, Jordan, Palestine, Tunisia, and the United States who participated in the Soliya Connect Program in 2011[13]. In this book, I spare readers the arduous task of reading through pages and pages of dense transcripts and analyses. I instead present the theoretical framework for exploring identity as it emerges in interaction and draw on some of the data and analyses from my study in order to illustrate how facilitator and participant identities emerged and were negotiated in this online situated context.

The first part of the book presents the theoretical framework and research approach adopted for the exploration of identity in this virtual exchange context. I first of all provide a brief overview (Chapter 2) of how language and identity have been conceptualised in foreign language education and in some online spaces. I then present the theoretical framework (Chapter 3), which is grounded in poststructuralist views of identity as social action and is specifically targeted at the study of identity in online interactions. It builds on

---

13. My full PhD study is available online at https://www.educacion.gob.es/teseo/mostrarRef.do?ref=1351668.

five key principles. These regard the **situatedness** of interaction and identity work; the **mediation** of technology in online interactions and identity work; and then three principles drawn from the work of Bucholtz and Hall (2005), **positionality**, **indexicality**, and **relationality**. In Chapter 4, I explain the rationale behind combining an interaction based approach broadly informed by conversation analysis with ethnography for an emic understanding of the interactional data. I then provide a description of the online context in which this study was based, the Soliya Connect Program, and explain my different positionings within it.

The second part of the book illustrates the application of the theoretical framework. All identity work takes place in situated contexts that shape – but do not determine – the identity positionings of the participants interacting in them. In Chapter 5, I begin with the 'situatedness principle' as I explore Soliya as an 'epistechnical system' (Williamson, 2013) in order to understand the factors that might have influenced the design of the Soliya Connect Program and the identities that are made relevant. All interaction and identity work is also mediated, but online interactions have an additional layer of complexity that should not be ignored. In Chapter 6, I look at the design features of the environments and technologies used for the interactions, the affordances and constraints of the different communication modalities available for identity work. I explore two different environments within Soliya, which is not an open social network but a protected, closed space. My starting point is the asynchronous, static, written, and visual modes of the Soliya blog, where participants first engage in identity work as they enter the platform. I then move to the meeting room where the synchronous audio-video dialogue sessions were held. In Chapters 7 and 8, I explore the situated identities of facilitators and participants, how their identities are co-constructed in their interactions in this situated, mediated space through positionality, indexicality and relationality. Shifting identity positionings influence interaction patterns as they can alter the power dynamics and have an impact on participants' investment in the dialogue process.

The aim of the book is not to provide a solution to the critical issues I have identified in the telecollaboration literature, nor is it intended to be a manual on virtual exchange or online facilitation. As virtual exchange is becoming an increasingly common educational approach[14], the intention of this book is to propose ways for exploring identities as they emerge in online interactions. The research-informed theoretical content of this work also has an applied focus in that better understanding the processes of identity formation in virtual exchange can lead to creating more effective uses of this educational practice.

---

14. In 2018 the European Commission launched the Erasmus+ Virtual Exchange pilot project, for example, aiming to offer experience of virtual exchange to 25,000 young people by the end of 2019; http://europa.eu/rapid/press-release_IP-18-1741_en.htm

Section 1.

A framework for analysing identity and interaction in online contexts

Identity, learning, and interaction

"I knew who I was this morning, but I've changed a few times since then"[1] (Carroll, 2000).

"Every time learners speak, listen, read, or write, they are not only engaged in an exchange of information; they are organizing and reorganizing a sense of who they are and how they relate to the social world. They are, in other words, engaged in identity construction and negotiation" (Norton, 1997, p. 410).

In recent years, identity has come to be recognised as complex and multilayered, fluid, and in constant flux (Block, 2007/2014; Bucholtz & Hall, 2005; Norton, 2000/2013; Norton Peirce, 1995; Norton & Toohey, 2011). Individuals are seen to perform and negotiate identities through actions and language, in multiple modes and in diverse times and spaces. Stemming from the social sciences and sparked by societal changes of 'globalisation', performative orientations to identity have fed into studies of language teaching and learning. These approaches challenge the assumptions which characterised the structuralist conceptualisations of language, culture, and identity that have characterised foreign language teaching (Firth & Wagner, 1997) and also intercultural education (Dervin, 2013; Dooly & Vallejo Rubinstein, 2017; Phipps, 2014; Piller, 2017).

In this chapter, I explore identity in relation to learning and interaction, with a particular focus on language learning – in part because of my background as a language teacher and researcher, and also due to a recognition of the limitations that the 'traditional' language classroom has offered in terms of identity positionings, as highlighted in the previous chapter. Having a greater

---

1. Alice's Adventures in Wonderland & Through the Looking-Glass; http://www.goodreads.com/work/quotes/2375385

understanding of identities and how they are negotiated in interaction and in educational contexts can, I believe, be of relevance to educators working in any context. Orientations to different identities can have a strong impact on power dynamics, student participation and the extent to which learning can take place.

2.1. Structuralist and poststructuralist views of language and identity

The Newtonian or Modernist view of the world as described in Chapter 1 can be found in structuralist conceptualisations of languages as static, bounded entities and systems, the acquisition of which entails mastery of stable patterns and structures. Linked to this are views of language as an aspect of individual cognition, which have dominated the field of second language acquisition. In their highly influential 1997 paper which critiqued this approach, Firth and Wagner (1997) note that "the imposition of an orthodox social psychological hegemony on second language acquisition has had the effect of reducing social identities to 'subjects', or at best to a binary distinction between natives and non-natives/learners" (p. 288). This has led to a preoccupation with the *learner* over other potentially relevant social identities.

The identity positions available to language learners in classrooms which embrace purely structuralist conceptualisations of language are quite limited and fixed. As Pennycook (2001) writes,

> "the issues of language learning have been cast as questions to do with the acquisition of morphemes, syntax, and lexis, with pronunciation or communicative competence, and the learner has been cast as a one-dimensional acquisition device. From this perspective, learners are viewed according to a mechanistic metaphor, as a sort of language learning machine, and identity-related issues are categorised as 'learner variables' which need to be 'controlled' in language learning contexts" (p. 143).

Whilst second language acquisition theory has certainly provided valuable insights into the way grammar is acquired and the role of formal instruction in language acquisition, it has little to say about the contexts of learning, language as social action, or learners as people with multiple identities. In language teaching, this focus on mastery of the system and an emphasis on grammar or vocabulary and correctness has led to approaches which emphasise linguistic knowledge and communicative competence rather than the expression of personal identities and meanings. Even the communicative language classroom encourages learners to become able to perform specific functions in communication contexts by learning and practising a repertoire of formulated, memorised textbook dialogues rather than authentic communication of their own interests (Ushioda, 2011).

On the other hand, poststructuralist theories (more in line with the complex systems view of the world described in Chapter 1) see language as a social phenomenon: situated utterances in which speakers seek to create meanings in dialogue with others. Drawing inspiration from Bakhtin (1986), according to whom language had no existence outside its use, language learning has come to be seen (by some) as a process of struggling to use language in order to participate in specific speech communities. Conceptualising language as usage sees speakers as being constrained in some ways by past usages to construct meaning, but also recognises their ability to use language to express their own meanings. This view of language is at the basis of poststructuralist conceptualisations of identity. Just as language and meaning making is viewed as a social phenomenon, so is the establishment of identity. Block (2007/2014) summarises poststructuralist framing of identity as follows:

> "Poststructuralist social scientists frame identities as socially constructed, self-conscious, ongoing narratives that individuals perform, interpret and project in dress, bodily movements, actions and language. Identity work occurs in the company of others – either [face to face] or in an electronically mediated mode – with whom to varying degrees individuals share beliefs, motives, values, activities and practices. Identities are about negotiating new subject positions at the crossroads of the past, present and future. Individuals are shaped

by their sociohistories but they also shape their sociohistories as life goes on. The entire process is conflictive as opposed to harmonious and individuals often feel ambivalent. There are unequal power relations to deal with, around the different capitals – economic, cultural and social, that both facilitate and constrain interactions with others in the different communities of practice with which individuals engage in their lifetimes. Finally identities are related to different traditionally demographic categories such as ethnicity, race, nationality, migration, social class and language" (p. 32).

As mentioned in the introduction, research on identity in language learning seeks to draw links between language learning and the larger social world. Poststructuralist theories of language and identity can offer new perspectives on language learning and teaching and offer a conceptualisation of the language learner as having "a complex social identity that must be understood with reference to large and frequently inequitable social structures which are reproduced in day-to-day social interactions" (Norton Pierce, 1995, p. 579).

2.2. Identity, subjectivities, and positioning

The origins of poststructuralist views of identity in language learning are generally attributed to the work of Chris Weedon (1987/1997), who used the term "subjectivities" to refer to "the conscious and unconscious thoughts and emotions of the individual, her sense of herself and her ways of understanding her relation in the world" (p. 28). In contrast to the essentialist, static view of identity in structural theories, Weedon's (1987/1997) subjectivity is "precarious, contradictory and in process, constantly reconstituted in discourse each time we think or speak" (p. 32).

Subjectivity makes reference to the way the subject positions herself and/or is positioned through discourse and is socially and historically embedded. It is thus dynamic, contradictory, and changes over time and space. The term subjectivity makes relevant the notion that individuals can simultaneously be the subject of a set of relationships (e.g. in a position of power) and subject **to** a set of relationships (e.g. in a position of reduced power). Weedon (1987/1997) observes that the adoption of subject positions, that is performances and positioning, does not take place in a vacuum. In a sense, the ongoing push and pull and give and take of discursive activity translates into the constant positioning and repositioning and the constant definition and redefinition of who one is (Block, 2007/2014, p. 24).

2.3. Locating identities in language

A framework for the analysis of identity as constituted in linguistic interaction, starting from the definition of identity as "the social positioning of self and other" is proposed by Bucholtz and Hall (2005, p. 586). They approach identity as "a relational and socio-cultural phenomenon that emerges and circulates in local discourse contexts of interaction rather than as a stable structure located primarily in the individual psyche or in fixed social categories" (Bucholtz & Hall, 2005, p. 586). Their work reflects the poststructuralist conceptualisation of identity as fluid and emergent, performed and negotiated through interactions with others in situated contexts, facilitated and constrained by power relations (Block, 2007/2014; Norton, 2000/2013; Norton Peirce, 1995). Their framework for an in-depth multi-dimensional study of identity as constituted in interaction draws insights from theorists in several fields including sociolinguistics, linguistic anthropology, socially oriented forms of discourse analysis, such as conversation analysis, and linguistically-oriented social psychology (Antaki & Widdicombe, 1998; Bucholtz, 1999, 2003; Bucholtz & Hall, 2004a, 2004b; Butler, 1990; Davies & Harré, 1990; Garfinkel, 1967; Goffman, 1974, 1981; Goodwin, 1995; Ochs, 1992, 1993).

If we take this sociocultural linguistic view, identity does not precede discourse in predefined, static, broad sociological categories such as nationality, race, or gender (to name but a few), but rather *emerges* within discourse and is achieved intersubjectively through interaction. This location of identity in discourse allows the incorporation of more identity *positionings* than the macro-categories mentioned above, as it also includes local ethnographic positionings, as defined by the situated context (for example student and teacher identities in classroom contexts). These situated identities are performed through discursive actions, for example teachers initiate interactions, students respond, and teachers evaluate responses and/or offer feedback. Identity is produced at these different levels through linguistic resources which *index* these positionings, for example labels, implicatures, stance, and even the use of specific languages and/or language varieties.

Viewing the construction of identity through interaction means it cannot be viewed as an individual process but rather as an intersubjective one, which entails different kinds of relations. The *relations* of sameness and difference have been the main focus in studies of intercultural interactions, but there are also relations of realness and fakeness, and power and disempowerment (Bucholtz & Hall, 2005, p. 608). Finally, associated with this emergent view of identity as constructed through interaction is the understanding that all representations of identity are necessarily *partial*, and dependent on interactional, ideological, and structuralist constraints. In any one interaction, only some of our identity categories are oriented to, for example when I go to a parents' evening at my children's school, it is usually my identity as a parent which is oriented to by my interactants, the teachers, not for example my professional, national, or political identities.

If identity is understood as discursively constructed and reconstituted every time we engage in interaction, it becomes clear how contexts and practices can limit opportunities for language learners to engage in language use. However, the opposite also holds, contexts and practices can surely be designed specifically to offer learners enhanced possibilities for social interaction and positioning. Pedagogical practices can be transformative in offering language learners more powerful positions than those they may occupy both within and outside the language classroom. Within the teacher-led language classroom, learners are often relegated to the position of respondent who answers teachers' questions and is then evaluated on the correctness of these responses (Richards, 2006). By offering different identity positionings, we can enable learners to engage in different discourses, advance beliefs, and challenge, defend, explain, and judge arguments. Technologies and the practice of virtual exchange have vastly increased the range of situated contexts available for identity work, and like face to face contexts, these can be constraining or enhancing.

2.4. Identity, investment, and language learning

The notion of investment (Darvin & Norton, 2015; Norton, 2000/2013; Norton & Williams, 2012) is an important construct from the identity and language learning literature which is potentially of great relevance to the field of virtual exchange. The notion of investment recognises that "learners often have variable desires to engage in the range of social interactions and community practices in which they are situated" (Norton, 2000/2013, p. 420). Norton (2000/2013) draws on Bourdieu's (1977, 1984, 1991) economic metaphors and notions such as capital and its exchange value as she observes that learners 'invest' in the target language in certain times and spaces because they see it as leading to the acquisition of symbolic and material resources which will increase the 'value' of their cultural 'capital' – and hence their sense of themselves. Investment and identity signal the "socially and historically constructed relationship of learners to the target language and their sometimes ambivalent desire to learn and practice it" (Norton Peirce, 1995, p. 9). According to Kramsch (2013), Norton's (2000/2013) adoption of the economic metaphor of investment suggests that the exchange value of learners' cultural capital is intrinsically linked to neoliberal conceptualisations of market value, in terms of employability and strategic economic possibilities. The frequent association of the notion of investment with the English language[2], often recognised as **the** language of neoliberalism (Piller & Cho, 2013), reinforces this link.

However researchers have shown that learners may invest in a language for a range of reasons. Individuals may invest in a language because it is a part of their heritage (Klimanova & Dembovskaya, 2013), or because they may see it as a tool

---

2. Norton Peirce (1995) developed the concept as she was doing research on immigrant English as a second language learners and she and other researchers usually refer to the English language when discussing investment (e.g. Darvin & Norton, 2015; Pavlenko & Norton, 2007) but research on the notion of investment has also been carried out as regards other languages, such as French (Bemporad & Jeanneret, 2016).

to spread knowledge about their culture and beliefs to those who do not speak their language. Individuals may invest in a language because it will allow them to communicate their shared needs and goals with national and transnational communities, as in the case of Rigoberta Menchu (1984), the Quiché indigenous leader who learnt Spanish to communicate with other indigenous communities in Guatemala and across Latin America. Individuals may also invest in a language because it is the "language of the enemy" (Pavlenko, 2003, p. 313, cited in Charalambous, 2014; Mohd-Asraf, 2005, p. 113).

2.5. Imagined identities

Strongly linked to the notion of investment is learners' membership in 'imagined communities' and hence imagined identities, which draws on Anderson's (1991) view of nation states as imagined communities. In their conceptualisation of imagined identities Pavlenko and Norton (2007) also draw on Wenger's (1998) conceptualisation of imagination as a form of engagement with communities of practice, and the notion of possible selves (Markus & Nurius, 1986), which represent individuals' conceptualisation of what they might become, what they would like to become, and what they are afraid of becoming. Imagined identities can affect individuals' learning trajectories and influence their agency, motivation, investment, and resistance to the learning of English, Pavlenko and Norton (2007) argue.

The English language may represent for some individuals a way to connect to a broader community – not necessarily of people in Anglophone countries, but rather English users – who share political, environmental, social, or leisure interests and concerns. At the same time, if we consider the experiences of many countries with colonialism, the imposition of English and the outlawing of other languages in certain contexts, the teaching of English as a missionary language (see Pennycook & Coutand-Marin, 2003), concerns about the loss of cultural values, identity and local languages (Mohd-Asraf, 2005) as a result of using English, we can understand how imagined identities might also invoke resistance to the language.

2.6. Online identities

Darvin and Norton (2015) have reviewed Norton's (2000/2013) model of identity and investment from a more global perspective, in acknowledgement of the "demands of the new world order, spurred by technology and characterized by mobility" (p. 35). This new model occurs "at the intersection of identity, ideology and capital" (Darvin & Norton, 2015, p. 36) and regards not only investment in (English) language, but also in digital literacies (Norton & Williams, 2012) which are seen to have expanded what is socially imaginable for learners and has extended the range of possible identities. Technological developments and increased mobility have increased the number and nature of spaces available to learners, and at the same time call for the ability to shift between different sets of communicative norms and power dynamics in spaces where power mechanisms are less and less visible. It is important, they argue, to interrogate ideologies and examine the sociopolitical contexts of schools and communities in order to examine how power manifests itself materially in the practices of a classroom or a community, in the positioning of interlocutors and the shifting values of linguistic and cultural capital.

Several scholars have reported on how online contexts give young people the chance to invest in and construct identities which are not available to them in their formal, monolingual classrooms (Chen, 2013; Iskold, 2012; Klimanova & Dembovskaya, 2013; Lam, 2000; McBride, 2009; Pasfield-Neofitou, 2011; Sauro, 2014; Schreiber, 2015; Sharma, 2012; Sykes, Oskoz, & Thorne, 2008; Thorne & Black, 2011). Most of this work on online identity construction has regarded the 'public agora' (Dervin, 2013) whereby learners interact in pre-existing online communities of practice, social networks such as Facebook, Vkontakte (for Russian), or Mixi (for Japanese), or fan fiction sites and online games.

Lam's (2000, 2006) study is one of the most-often cited studies in relation to online identities and language learning (Kramsch, 2009; Norton & Toohey, 2011). She explores the ways in which technology provides language learners with the means to construct imagined lives by examining the computer-mediated transnational identities that immigrant youth in the USA were fashioning for themselves as multilingual, multicompetent actors. She found that these identities afforded broader opportunities for language learning than their school environment where they were stigmatised as immigrants and incompetent language users. Lam concludes that identity issues for teachers and learners are significant factors in the philosophical, pedagogical, and professional domains of language teaching.

Identity work and empowerment has become one of the main themes in research into online or computer-mediated fan fiction practices (Sauro, 2017). Black's (2009) case studies describe how adolescent writers of English as a second language chose to represent themselves not as learners of English, but rather as transcultural and multilingual writers who were a source of linguistic and cultural expertise. Sauro (2017) highlights how through fan engagement in online settings, L2 learners and users are "able to renegotiate new and more productive multilingual and international identities, and confront and challenge social issues and dominant discourses" (p. 141).

What seems to emerge from the literature on online identities for language learners is the increased opportunities for identity positionings that arise from becoming part of a group or community which has a shared interest or aim. As research into communities of practice (Wenger, 1998) has found, social participation means being active participants in the practices of social communities and constructing identities, (actual or imagined) in relationship to these communities. Positionality in online groups or communities has been explored through the *Community of Inquiry* framework (Garrison, Anderson, & Archer, 2000) and more recently the *Community Indicators* framework (Galley, Conole, & Panagiota, 2014; Hauck, Galley, & Warnecke, 2016). Identity is one of the four components of the *Community Indicators* framework which also includes participation, cohesion and creative capability as indicators of community.

A framework for the study of identity in online interactions through virtual exchange

In this chapter, I propose a theoretical framework for the study of identity in interaction that is grounded in the poststructuralist views of identity as social action that I explored in the previous chapter. It is specifically targeted for the study of identity in online interactions and builds on five key principles. These include the **situatedness** of interaction and identity work; the **mediation** of technology in online interactions and identity work; and three principles drawn from the work of Bucholtz and Hall (2005); **positionality**, **indexicality**, and **relationality**. These principles are explained briefly in this chapter, and then each will be explored in further detail in subsequent chapters, drawing on examples from the study of interactions in a specific context of virtual exchange.

3.1. The situatedness principle

"Emerging arrays of online environments now constitute primary settings through which routine constructions of identity are created, and curated, through the use of textual and multimodal expression, some of which arguably involve new literacies, communicative genres, hybrid linguistic varieties, processes of group formation, and social practices" (Thorne, Sauro, & Smith, 2015, p. 216).

The virtual space called the web has been recognised as the largest language contact zone and social space on earth, a new sociological and anthropological reality which presents challenges to the analyst who needs to depart from the anachronistic mode of analysis which characterises much research on social networks (Blommaert & de Fina, 2015). The range of transnational spaces of communication are varied and are constantly changing, so they need to be continually studied to understand the changing contexts of language and/in social life (e.g. Herring, 2007; Thorne, 2016). Often, the sites of digital language and literacy in the ecology of multilingual environments that the internet offers are merely mentioned rather than studied in the research literature (see though Androutsopoulos & Juffermans, 2014; Lam, 2014; Sundqvist & Sylvén, 2014).

The principle of situatedness stems from the field of ethnography, according to which "the distinction between linguistic and nonlinguistic is an artificial one since every act of language needs to be situated in wider patterns of human social behavior, and intricate connections between various aspects of this complex need to be specified" (Blommaert, 2015, p. 8). In analysing interaction in online sites, we cannot ignore the contexts and purposes for which the spaces themselves were designed (educational, recreational, commercial, social, political, etc.) and the purposes for which they may be used by the different communities. Online contexts of interaction are "socially constructed and historically contingent" (Williamson, 2013, p. 40), they are *socially shaped* and *socially shaping*. Virtual learning environments such as Moodle, Blackboard, and many more were designed for educational contexts and are shaped by (Western) educational models which see a strong need for providing (limited) access to teacher-selected academic content and controlling, monitoring, assessing and grading the structured and sequenced activities of students.

Social networks, on the other hand, have been designed for 'creating connections' between people – as is well known, Facebook was launched as a social network for Harvard University, initially to connect students to one another. It has since evolved above all for commercial ends – and is highly profitable if we consider that its net annual income for 2017 was over 15 billion dollars[1]. Facebook's design was shaped by the context within which it was born and has grown, and it is also socially shaping – the main functions, 'liking' and 'sharing' are designed to foster convergence and the sharing of content amongst the like-

---

1. https://www.statista.com/statistics/277229/facebooks-annual-revenue-and-net-income/

minded, with the 'help' of targeted Facebook ads which are directed to us on the basis of knowledge that Facebook has acquired (and sold) through our web surfing habits. The interactions of communities within Facebook are also likely to index events which occur outside the timespace of their online group, both in the individual lives of the participants but also on a more global level. The online and the offline times and spaces thus interact with and shape one another.

According to Herring (2007), aspects – or facets – which should be taken into account when describing the situated contexts of online interactions include the purpose of the group and the goals of interaction; the participation structure, which includes the degrees of privacy, the membership in terms of numbers of participants, the directionality of the communication (one-to-many, many-to-many); and the characteristics of the participants and their roles in the online space. However, what is missing from these 'facets' that Herring (2007) has defined are macro-level situational factors, linked to the ideologies and the sociopolitical nature of online contexts that may also shape interactions and participant positionings within these, as discussed above.

If we look at educational contexts and 'educational technology' (Selwyn & Facer, 2013) we should consider them as a site of negotiation and struggle between different actors (Bourdieu & Passeron, 1990), which include the designers and developers of new tools and curricula, consultants, funders and advocates, as well as the young people that the educational projects are addressing, their families and communities. They should be explored on a 'macro' level of social structure of society as well as the microlevel of the individual and the learning context.

3.2. The mediation principle

"Artifacts and humans together create particular morphologies of action" (Thorne, 2016, p. 189).

Whilst all discourse is mediated, in electronic environments, discourse, and hence identity work, takes on additional layers of mediation, with a technological layer of operations in addition to the social interactional layer. This principle challenges the notion that technology is a neutral or transparent medium for communication and identity work and instead sees mediation as radically transforming these and other social processes (Kern, 2014, 2015).

As stated in Helm (2017, p. 8), taking for granted the existence of the Internet and its effects on communication, and indeed education, is reductionist and fails to take into account the multiple forms of online mediated activity; the contexts of the creation, development, uses, and transformations of technologies and their mediating effect. Kramsch and Thorne (2002) raise this very issue as they ask the extent to which the medium changes the parameters of communication and the nature of language use (see also Blommaert, 2015; Thorne, 2013). The mediating effect of technologies and the affordances they offer cannot be ignored in the analysis of online interactions (Hampel & Hauck, 2006).

The first assumption within the mediation principle is that all interaction is multimodal (see Kern, 2015, p. 223), not just technology-mediated interactions. *Multimodality* "makes sensory information accessible in diverse semiotic modes and offers the opportunity to produce, comprehend and exchange information simultaneously through different channels" (Guichon & Cohen, 2016, p. 510). However, sometimes the additional mediating layers of technology can create dislocations for participants in interaction who need to negotiate the technological as well as linguistic, social, and/or intercultural aspects of interaction (Kern, 2015).

What technologies have added are new modalities and media for communication. Different media can facilitate or favour different kinds of meaning making and identity work (Bezemer & Jewitt, 2010); media can also constrain communication through the design of the tools themselves and the differential access to the means of production and reception of these meanings. An important concept within this principle is 'affordance', which stems from ecological theory. It refers to the relationship between properties of the environment and the active learner. An affordance is a particular property of the environment that allows for further action. In language learning, the environment the learner has access to and in which they become engaged is "full of demands and requirements, opportunities and limitations, rejections and invitations, enablements and constraints – in short, affordances (Shotter & Newson, 1982, p. 34)" (van Lier, 2000, p. 253).

What was originally seen as an affordance of text-based computer-mediated communication for identity work is the anonymity it allows, for visual identity markers disappear. The well known adage, which stems from the cartoon by Peter Steiner *On the Internet nobody knows you're a dog*[2] – reflects what some saw as the liberatory power in terms of self representation and identity construction that the (perceived) anonymity of text-based communication offered.

The affordances of anonymity in computer-mediated communication have, in the public sphere, been overrun by the negative effects that the lack of accountability has offered for hate speech and abuse. It is not only the anonymity, but also other factors that contributed to what has been called the *Online Disinhibition Effect*[3] and these include invisibility, asynchronicity, and what is called 'solipsistic introjection', that is the fact that you can't actually see your interactants online and thus have to guess at who they are and their intent.

Recent technology developments have strongly affected mediation in online contexts. Audio and video are increasingly being used for everyday communication, and also in educational contexts, with multiple modes of communication being available in any one environment, and users being required to navigate and negotiate these modes through different devices and interfaces. The implications of video and aural communication for identity work are significant since anonymity disappears through video, and visual identity markers are available to interactants. The audio mode of communication also introduces identity markers such as accents, which text-based communication does not transparently reveal.

---

2. https://en.wikipedia.org/wiki/On_the_Internet,_nobody_knows_you%27re_a_dog

3. http://www.wired.co.uk/article/online-aggression

The emergence and phenomenal success of social networking sites have somewhat changed the dynamics and attitudes towards anonymity in online identity work because their main aim is for users to curate their identities and their personal, social and/or professional networks. The importance of mediation can also be seen in the construction and negotiation of identities online, with much of the recent research focussing on the affordances of social networking sites and multimodal media used for engaging in 'identity work' (boyd, 2006). The aims of the social networking site, the conventions developed for communication within the network itself, and the technical affordances of the tools influence the message and the identities that are mediated through these tools.

3.3. The positionality principle

> "Identities encompass (a) macrolevel demographic categories; (b) local, ethnographically specific cultural positions; and (c) temporary and interactionally specific stances and participant roles" (Bucholtz & Hall, 2005, p. 592).

This principle challenges the notion that identity is simply a collection of broad social categories, those macro-identity categories such as age, gender and social class, which have dominated the quantitative social science literature and early sociolinguistic work. It brings in a concern with how identity relations arise in local contexts and draws on the work of linguistic ethnographers regarding how language users orient to local identity categories and also the micro details of identity as it emerges through interactional positionings.

These different levels of identity positionings, which are not mutually exclusive, have been conceptualised by several theorists, but in this book I draw in particular on the work of Zimmerman (1998), who distinguished between transportable, situated, and discourse identities. Transportable identities refer to identity categories which are commonly recognisable across large groups, such as 'female', 'young person', 'Muslim'. Situated identities are those local, ethnographically specific cultural positions which are somehow institutionally existent, such as teachers and students, doctors and patients and, in the context of this book, facilitators and participants. Finally, discourse identities correspond to interactionally specific stances and participant roles, for example questioner – respondent, speaker – and listener.

These three levels of identity positionings are not unrelated, nor do they occur in isolation, but can occur simultaneously in single interactions. Most research studies in this field have explored the correspondence between discourse and situated identities, particularly in institutional contexts. According to Boden and Zimmerman (1991),

> "[t]he structure of institutional talk minimally consists of the recurrent pattern of normatively oriented-to, situated identities along with the corresponding discourse identities and the conversational machinery through which the work allotted to participants assuming such identities is done. In the case of television news interviews, for example, interviewer-interviewee are the oriented-to identities which allocate (and constrain) certain discourse activities, e.g. asking questions and giving answers" (p. 13).

Richards (2006), who has used Zimmerman's (1998) framework to study identities in classroom interactions, argues that most research studies on classroom interaction take the default identities of teacher and student for granted. Furthermore he found that these default, situated identities offer little scope for moving outside of what could be seen as the default pattern of classroom interaction: initiation, response, and feedback. In the excerpts that Richards (2006) first analyses, it is the teacher who takes on the discourse identity of initiator and has the authority to control the floor, ask questions, give instructions, and prompt, while the students (aka respondents) are expected to respond directly to these turns and address the teacher. The teacher is also the evaluator and provider of feedback or follow-ups which can take on many forms (positive evaluation or remedial action such as explicit correction, clarification requests, repetition, and reformulation to name but a few).

In his study, Richards (2006) then analyses interactions in which students' transportable identities are brought into play, and he argues that this offers opportunities for subverting the *initiation-response-feedback* dynamic as students are engaged in a conversation where they are actively involved in the construction of shared understanding. Richards' (2006) main claim is that introducing transportable identity in the language classroom – both of teachers and students, can redress power dynamics and transform the sort of interaction that takes place in the classroom.

Many other studies have explored classroom interactions and indeed the *initiation-response-feedback* pattern has been found to predominate (cf. Hall & Walsh, 2002; Heritage, 2005; Seedhouse, 2009). In telecollaboration studies where interaction patterns have been explored (Liddicoat & Tudini, 2013; Loizidou & Mangenot, 2016), similar findings have been made, only it is usually the 'native speaker' student who takes on the 'teacher/tutor' identity by providing feedback on the 'non-native' peer's 'errors'. A recent study by Dooly and Tudini (2016) on the other hand found that in a dyadic pair of student-teachers, the non-native peer took on the role of teacher/tutor more frequently than the native speaker, in regards to 'guiding' the online talk. The pedagogic discursive practices discussed thus far are but some of the many forms of interaction an active user of a language will engage with once outside of the classroom. Indeed, it is argued that these institutionally situated pedagogic interactions can potentially disempower learners, constraining their agency to obedience and limited participation (Train, 2006).

Telecollaboration 'in the wild' (Thorne, 2010), whereby language learners interact in pre-existing online communities, offers increased opportunities for identity positionings that encourage participants to seek to become members of authentic, online communities of practice. These communities can include public internet discussion forums (Hanna & de Nooy, 2003, 2009; Lam, 2006), fanfiction sites, virtual worlds, gaming sites, and social networks (Thorne, Sauro, & Smith, 2015). The increased opportunities for building socially meaningful relationships and identities arise from becoming part of a group or community which has a shared interest or aim. In these settings, participants work to position themselves as 'members', and particular uses and forms of language that are central or specific to the target community form the primary resources for doing so.

3.4. The indexicality principle

"Identity relations emerge in interaction through several related indexical processes, including (a) overt mention of identity categories and labels; (b) implicatures and presuppositions regarding one's own or others' identity position; (c) displayed evaluative and epistemic orientations to ongoing talk, as well as interactional footings and participants' roles; and (d) the use of linguistic structures and systems that are ideologically associated with specific personas and groups" (Bucholtz & Hall, 2005, p. 594).

This principle regards the multiple levels at which subjectivity and intersubjectivity can be constituted in interaction. An index is essentially a linguistic form that depends on the interactional context for its meaning, such as the first person pronoun 'I', 'the', 'here' (etc.), and temporal expressions such as 'now' (often referred to as deictic words in semantics). However, indexicality also regards the linking of linguistic forms and social meanings and the ideological structures on which identity formation is often based, and is far less clear-cut than semantic indexicality, as the very word implicature implies.

Social category labels (such as age, gender, ethnicity) have been used in the study of identity primarily by non-linguistically focussed social science researchers, but linguistic researchers also have a long history of attention to this area. Table 3.1, below, summarises the categories which key research on language and identity have focussed on. Taken-for-granted categories of identity (some can be described in a single word such as gender, class, and nationality, while others are more complex to define) are seen to reflect structural conditions and established social practices. These identity categories can be used (and abused) to position people, to empower and/or disempower them. From a poststructuralist view, established identity categories can be made relevant but also ignored through interaction; they can be challenged and negotiated.

Table 3.1. Identity categories in studies of identity

Norton (2000/2013)	Pavlenko and Blackledge (2004)	Block (2007/2014)
• Ethnicity	• Ethnicity and nationality	• Race and ethnicity
• Class	• Gender	• National identity
• Gender	• Race	• Migrant identity
• Language and communicative competence	• Class and social status	• Gender
	• Able bodiedness	• Social class
	• Sexuality	• Language (Second/foreign)
	• Religious affiliation	
	• Linguistic competence and ability to claim a 'voice'	

Socio-cultural linguistic researchers, including those mentioned above, but also those more focussed on the study of interaction, have offered more systematic methodologies for understanding labelling and categorisation as social action. The work of Harvey Sacks (1992) on membership categorisation in conversation, and its development in the two related but distinct ethnomethodological approaches of *conversation analysis* and *membership categorisation analysis* (Stokoe, 2012) regard categories and labels both through their overt mention but also the assumed behaviour and attributes of category members.

Bucholtz and Hall (2005) draw on the work of du Bois (2007), who interprets stance as both a subjective and intersubjective phenomenon and characterises it as social action. In this view, a subject takes a stance by evaluating something, positioning themselves and others, and aligning – or disaligning – with other subjects. Positioning oneself is thus a component of taking a stance. Looking at stance thus reveals how interactants position themselves and others ("I evaluate something, and thereby position myself, and align [or disalign] with you" (du Bois, 2007, p. 163) as particular types of people.

Many public online discussion forums, particularly those where issues that are closely intertwined with identity (such as migration), are characterised by adversarial positionings and 'flaming' with polarised discussions and comments removed by moderators. On the other hand, in online intercultural exchange, there has been a strong influence of the notions of 'sociocultural competence' and an emphasis on alignment with the other, to the point of dissimulating one's own point of view (Savignon & Sysoyev, 2002). In the telecollaboration literature, researchers have identified a tension between fear of 'failed communication' due to misunderstandings which lead to the preliminary termination of communication between peers, and 'missed communication' (Ware, 2005), that is missed opportunities for deeper engagement with one another due to superficial communication.

According to Bucholtz and Hall (2005), entire linguistic systems such as languages and dialects as well as particular linguistic forms can be indexically tied to identity categories. They cite the issue of language choice, which has been studied in the field of language and globalisation, and is perhaps one of the most explored constructs in studies in the field of language and identity (Higgins, 2009; Lee & Norton, 2009; Pavlenko & Blackledge, 2004).

3.5. The relationality principle

> "Identities are intersubjectively constructed through several, often overlapping, complementary relations, including similarity/difference, genuineness/artifice and authority/delegitimacy" (Bucholtz & Hall, 2005, p. 598).

This principle emphasises that "identities are never autonomous or independent but always acquire social meaning in relation to other available identity positions and other social actors" (Bucholtz & Hall, 2005, p. 598). This relational foundation of identity as opposed to the conception of identity as an inherently individual, psychological trait is what Bucholtz and Hall (2005) see as being at the heart of their model. Hanna and de Nooy (2009) highlight the relevance of this principle in their study of online discussion forums as they write "forum discussion [...] is not a game of solitaire where one's strategies can be adopted without reference to other players but rather a game where self-positioning also depends on that of the other participants in the debate" (p. 154).

The dimensions of this principle of relationality go beyond sameness and difference which are the most widely-used and also over simplified identity relations. Bucholtz and Hall (2005) have added other dimensions which relate to realness and fakeness, and power and disempowerment. These different dimensions, they argue, typically work in conjunction with one another.

Adequation and distinction are the terms used by Bucholtz and Hall (2005) to refer to relations of similarity and difference from which they draw, but also depart from. These are not dichotomous relations, same or different, but rather represent a continuum. The term adequation is used to refer to the foregrounding of similarities and the downplaying of social differences which might undermine or support identity work. It means being "understood as sufficiently similar for current interactional purposes" (Bucholtz & Hall, 2005, p. 599), it does not entail being identical. Distinction on the other hand refers to the suppression of similarities and allows for the construction of difference. If I say "Oh yes, I am a religious person" to somebody who has told me they go to the mosque every day, I am engaging in adequation, highlighting a degree of similarity with that person, though I do not belong to the same religion. If on the other hand I say "I am a Catholic and have never been into a mosque", I emphasise distinction and highlight difference. There are occasions on which and, more importantly reasons why, a speaker may choose to focus on difference, and others in which adequation is preferred, depending on the contingencies of the situation. It is important to be aware that reducing differences to similarities has often been used to dominate or silence others (Agbaria & Cohen, 2000; hooks, 1994).

Authentication and denaturalisation are the terms used for claims made by interactants to realness and artifice. Authentication regards how identities are discursively verified, and how the language users and the types of language they use counts as 'genuine' for a given purpose. Authentication occurs when fellow members of a community of practice accept the symbolic behaviour of an individual as appropriate and 'real', and this is expressed through participants orienting to one another. In her study of keypal interactions, Klimanova (2013) found that expression of genuine interest in various aspects of Russian language and culture was considered a form of self-proclaimed peripheral belonging to a Russian speakers' community. Self-identification as deficient speakers of Russian, which solidified their Russian learner identities, allowed novices to save face and mitigate their linguistic deficiencies and cultural faux-pas and be accepted by their interactants. Denaturalisation on the other hand, regards the claims made to artifice, how assumptions regarding the seamlessness of identity can be disrupted. Through denaturalisation, claims about inherent rightness of identities are subverted and attention is called to the fragmentation or problematicity of identity. In Hanna and de Nooy's (2009) study of discussion forums and sites specifically established for language learning (such as those of the BBC), they found that these sites set up default identities of language learners and teachers which replicate the default positions of the classroom context. These positions determined the topics and mode of discourse according to a small number of well-rehearsed patterns, but offered little scope for deep discussion on topics other than the learners themselves. One participant reported in their study attempted to denaturalise this learner identity which was ascribed to participants and to start a discussion on student protests, but the other participants on the forum oriented only to the language (i.e. errors) of her posts (which, the authors write, was well up to the task) rather than engage with the topic proposed (Hanna & de Nooy, 2009, p. 141) and thus did not authenticate her intentional and intended identity.

The final pair of identity relations takes into consideration structural and institutional aspects of identity that are enacted through contextually established situated identities. First of all, we have authorisation which is the "affirmation or imposition of an identity through structures of institutionalised power and ideology, whether local or translocal" (Bucholtz & Hall, 2005, p. 603). Its counterpart, illegitimisation, regards the ways in which these same power structures dismiss, censor, or ignore identities.

These latter pairs of relations can also be linked, I would argue, to the concept of communities of practice, which informs some of the research carried out on identity and language learning, for it shares the assumption that learning is situated in our lived experience and is a fundamentally social phenomenon. As identity formation is fundamentally a social and relational process, agency also needs to be understood as a fundamentally socioculturally mediated capacity to act (Ahearn, 2001). In this sense, agency is intersubjective, that is, it is not only the result of individual action, but distributed among several social actors. The *Communities of Practice* framework, and others which regard communities, thus offer potential in understanding the notion of distributed agency and joint activity or co-construction. As Norton and Toohey (2002) write:

> "a shift from seeing learners as individual language producers to seeing them as members of social and historical collectivities, moves observers toward examining the conditions for learning, for appropriation of practices, in any particular community" (p. 119).

If we conceive these communities as aggregates of people who come together to engage with the practices of their communities, in which there are ways of doing things and ways of talking, it is the community that offers authentication and denaturalisation, authorisation, and illegitimisation of participants' identities.

In Lave and Wenger's (1991) conceptualisation, communities of practice are not just groups of individuals but rather they are social aggregates that have and impose rules of entry. Individuals gain entry to communities of practice by means of "legitimate peripheral participation", which is achieved via exposure to "mutual engagement with other members, to their actions, and their negotiation of the enterprise, and to their repertoire in use" (Wenger, 1998, p. 101). This conceptualisation may be useful for already established communities that novices enter, as in Hanna and de Nooy's (2009) study, but is slightly less so for new groups that are established online. A more recent framework has been developed for the analysis of the emergence of online communities, which includes identity as a category, the *Community Indicators* framework (Hauck, Galley, & Warnecke, 2016). Within this framework, establishing limits, boundaries, purposes, and expectations is a component of the group identity, as are shared vocabulary, group self-awareness, and identification of existing knowledge and experience patterns.

An ethnographic interaction-based study

In the previous chapter, I described a theoretical framework that could be adopted for the study of identities in online contexts such as virtual exchange projects, but I did not dwell on methodological considerations. In this chapter, I outline the methodological orientation adopted for the in-depth study which the rest of the book is based on. I then provide a brief description of the context of the study and my positionings within it.

Androutsopoulos (2008) endorses Discourse-Centred Online Ethnography (DCOE), that is, the use of ethnography to supplement and support the linguistic analysis of interaction. In his view, "DCOE uses ethnographic insights as a backdrop to the selection, analysis and interpretation of log data, in order to illuminate relations between digital texts and their production and reception practices" (Androutsopoulos, 2008, p. 2), that is, broadening the scope of interpretation beyond what the transcripts alone could account for (Deppermann, 2000, in Androutsopoulos, 2008, p. 17).

In their 'pure' forms, the ethnographic and the interaction-based approaches can be seen as quite distinct from one another. Ethnographers use a wide range of data collecting instruments such as participant observation and interviews in order to provide a description of social settings and to capture aspects of members' life worlds. However, those working strictly in the tradition of conversation analysis, one of the more widely-used interaction-based approaches, do not take context into consideration. For them, the 'organised sequence of turns' in which an utterance appears is sufficient as the context of recognisable social actions. This strong version of conversation analysis "eschews ethnographic description because it draws on resources that are external to the participants' ongoing or real-time situated talk" (Maynard, 2006, p. 58).

Ethnographers critique conversation analysis for its avoidance of field methods and its deliberate neglect of social structure, unless of course social structures of various kinds are oriented to as relevant by participants within the interaction. However, researchers in the fields of discourse analysis (van Dijk, 1985), linguistically-oriented anthropology (Duranti, 1997; Goodwin, 1990; Gumperz, 1982), and sociology (Miller, 1994; Silverman, 1993) have been using recordings together with ethnographic methods – sometimes to supplement participant observation and interviews and sometimes without prioritising either approach (Maynard, 2006). These different approaches can be used with varying relations of affinity. Maynard (2006), for example, regards ethnography as an ineluctable resource for analysis but uses it with limited affinity, that is to provide analytic control over the interpretive statements.

With the increased interest in online interaction and identity work, researchers have been bringing the two closer together, and exploring how ethnography can provide greater access and understanding of the contexts of interaction. Given the vast range of online environments, the variety of mediating tools and the affordances and constraints that they place on interaction and identity work, it would perhaps be misleading and reductionist to rely on interaction data alone. As the theoretical framework discussed in the previous chapter highlights in the principles of situatedness and mediation, all online interaction is situated in an intentionally designed context and is mediated by technologies, both of which have some influence on the interactions taking place.

This study lies within the ethnographic tradition in that it is a qualitative study which seeks to provide a detailed, in-depth description (a 'thick description', Geertz, 1973) of a sociocultural context and the interactions that take place within it. Ethnographic understanding is acquired through close exploration of different sources of data, and also through participant observation and long-term engagement in the 'field', that is, the setting studied (Hoey, 2014).

The context of this study is an online community which I have engaged with for over eight years in various guises (described in the following section). What I seek to represent is the *emic* perspective, the 'insider's point of view', with categories and meanings emerging from the data and my understanding of the context rather than from a pre-existing, outside model.

This insider knowledge and understanding of the context which I have acquired over the years allows for an ethnographic approach, yet at the same time I have sought to take a distance from the context and approach it with a critical lens in order to explore the power relations that are constituted within this site. As in all situated contexts, there are structural affordances both within and outside the site which influence the identity work that takes place within it. There is thus a duality in this study (which indeed characterises all ethnographic work) for whilst I have been a participant in the context which I study, I also try to 'detach' myself from it and take on the stance of the observer and analyst of interactions. Hoey (2014) writes that

> "[g]iven that so much of ethnographic fieldwork depends on the researcher's own experience and perspective – i.e., the 'I' must be acknowledged – it really does matter where you as that researcher 'stand' relative to the process of your own fieldwork and ultimately to the subject of your study. That means not only whether or not you might consider yourself an 'insider' or an 'outsider' to a group that may be your focus but also the attitudes and/or preconceptions that you bring to that study" (p. 4).

I therefore begin this chapter by providing a brief description of the online environment in which this semi-ethnographic study has been carried out, then I outline my different positionings and identities as regards this context.

4.1. The online context of this study

The Soliya Connect Program was set up in 2003 by the American non-governmental organisation, Soliya. The founding members were Liza Chambers, with a background in conflict management and youth dialogue, and Lucas Welch, with a background in media production and teaching media.

Established in the aftermath of 9/11, the main aim of the program developers – as written on the website – was to bridge the gap between 'Western' and 'predominantly Muslim' societies, a gap widened by tensions which media representations were serving mainly to exacerbate. In order to do this, they designed a curriculum, drawing on their backgrounds in conflict transformation and dialogue, media production, and in consultation with experts in the field and academics from partner universities.

This curriculum formed the basis of the Soliya Connect Program, which since then has run twice a year, once in the spring semester and once in the fall semester, and involves partner universities who integrate the programme into their institutional courses in various ways. As the programme has evolved, two 'strands' developed, one focussing more on academic/political issues, and the other less academic and more intercultural, and several different versions of the programme targeted different audiences.

Originally, partner universities were based in the United States and the Middle East and North Africa, reflecting its original need and aims. Gradually, the geographic scope of the programme has expanded and Soliya began to include universities in Europe and other largely Muslim countries such as Pakistan and Indonesia in the Connect Program. To date, the Connect Program has been implemented in over 100 universities in more than 30 countries. The main goals of the Connect Program regard the spheres of understanding, relationship building, skill-building, and promoting change, as defined in the Soliya Curriculum (Soliya, 2010).

4.1.1. What are the goals of the Connect Program?

The goals of the Connect Program are clearly defined in the facilitator guide (Soliya, 2010):

> "Connect Program provides an opportunity for students to share their voices. Through this exchange we aim to accomplish the following objectives:

Understanding:
- Gain understanding of and empathy for the perspective/narrative of others in the group – not only the positions taken or the opinions expressed, but the core issues, the underlying assumptions, values, needs, and fears.
- Develop a clearer understanding of our own perspective, assumptions, values, identity, etc., as well as one's personal relationship with the issues.
- Gain understanding on each other's cultures and daily lives.

Relationship-building:
- Develop positive personal relationships with one another – not necessarily friendships, but relationships of mutual respect and understanding.

Skill-building:
- Cross cultural communication and collaboration.
- Critical thinking.
- Media literacy.
- Dignity-based approach to difference.

Change:
- Our hope is that all participants will have the opportunity to genuinely re-examine and analyse pre-existing opinions and beliefs in a space in which transformation and reconsideration of existing views is possible".

4.1.2. How does Soliya set out about reaching its aims?

Each semester, professors sign up for an institutional partnership with Soliya in which an agreement is made regarding the number of students that will participate and from which courses they will enroll. The number of student participants every year has gradually been growing, from several hundreds of students[1] to over 1000 at the time of writing. Each student participant creates their individual blogs in the Soliya Community area and then participates in a synchronous audio-video online facilitated dialogue for eight weeks as a member of a small dialogue group. Students may participate as a compulsory part of a curricular course they are following, as an optional component, or a stand-alone module. How the Connect Program is integrated into a university course, and how it is evaluated depends on the professor who registered their class for the Soliya Connect Program. For many students in the US, for example, it is a component of courses in conflict resolution, cross-cultural communication, or media studies, and it is an integral part of their courses. In my context (Political Science Department of the University of Padova), it is offered as an alternative to traditional classroom-based advanced English courses, and students have regular seminars about the project and written assignments (Helm, 2014).

There are currently over a hundred different dialogue groups each semester, led by different facilitators, but all the groups follow a shared calendar and curriculum. This shared curriculum was an intentional design feature to meet the requirements of universities who need some consistency in the programme in order to include it as an accredited part of their courses. A list of goals are defined for each week, and certain activities and topics are carried out over the course of the semester, other activities and topics are defined by the groups themselves. Facilitators use the Online Curriculum, a large resource pack with a series of activities they can select from for each of the themes and goals to be addressed each week. Within this framework and with the support of these resources, facilitators have the flexibility to address issues that their group identifies as important and to introduce activities that they feel will work well for their group.

Below is the calendar with the topics for discussion and suggested activities for the 2011 iteration of the Connect Program which was the object of this study.

Week 1 of the online dialogue. Topics that will be discussed:
- Introduction to group members and the online dialogue process.

---

1. This varies from semester to semester. It has expanded from 200 to over 1000 at the time of writing.

- Introduction to *Identity and Culture*: students participate in activities that enable them to explore identity issues and share cultural information.
- Identification of topics that students want to discuss.

Week 2 of the online dialogue. Topics that will be discussed:
- Investigating the nature of the relationship readings.
- What is the nature of the problem?
- What are 'Western societies'? What are 'predominantly Muslim societies'?
- After defining (or problematising) these terms, students outline what their community understands to be the root of the conflict between 'Western societies' and 'predominantly Muslim societies'
- **Discussion will be based upon the required readings for this week.**

Week 3 of the online dialogue. Topics that will be discussed:
- Culture and background: students will engage in activities enabling them to get to know one another and one another's backgrounds better.
- Investigating nature of the relationship. Follow your students' suggestions. Some topics that can work well are: immigration/integration, foreign policy, extremism, social movements, etc.

Week 4 of the online dialogue. Topics that will be discussed:
- Investigating the role of religion in society and students' lives.
- What role does religion play in your life? What role does religion play in your society?
- Does religion play a role in politics? What role does religion play in the politics of 'Western societies' versus 'predominantly Muslim societies'?
- The pair activity is highly recommended this week.

- **Discussion will be based upon the required readings for this week**

Week 5 of the online dialogue. Topics that will be discussed:
- Culture and background: students will engage in activities enabling them to get to know one another and one another's backgrounds better.
- Exploring the connection between the personal and the political through the *Life Stories* activity.

Week 6 of the online dialogue. Topics that will be discussed:
- Investigating the nature of the relationship: media.
- Discussion of the video projects.

Week 7 of the online dialogue. Topics that will be discussed:
- Working for change: group members formulate ideas as to what they can do individually and as a group to promote improved relations between 'Western societies' and 'predominantly Muslim societies'.
- Reflecting on the group process and ending the semester on a positive note.

4.2. Researcher positioning within the context

I first heard about the Soliya Connect Program when reading an academic paper about telecollaboration by Julie Belz (2007). I looked for the website, and read more about the Connect Program, which seemed like the ideal telecollaboration project to offer students in the department where I teach at the University of Padova, the Department of Political Science, Law, and International studies. I therefore wrote to Soliya asking whether and how I could have students participate. I received a positive response, inviting me to have a small group of students participate in the programme and subsequently signed up on the Soliya website as a *professor* and enrolled eight students as participants. I asked these students to write reflective diaries in the form of blogs about their experience of Soliya, which I regularly read, and had seminars every two to three weeks with the students to discuss their experience and progress. I was so struck by the impact that I could see this exchange having on students as I read their reflective journals that I too wanted to experience the Connect Program. In response to my request to participate in the following round of Soliya, I was invited to enrol in the facilitator training programme (for the exchange itself is generally limited to students) through which I could learn more and possibly progress to facilitating a group.

I thus entered the Soliya Connect Program with a new 'hat', that of *facilitator trainee*, and completed the eight week online facilitation training. Soon after I was offered my first *co-facilitator* assignment with a dialogue group. At the time of facilitating, however, I was not planning to do a PhD, so I did not approach the facilitation with an ethnographer's eye, but rather as an apprentice facilitator. Since then I have facilitated several groups, and have also had the opportunity to become a Soliya *coach*. Soliya coaches serve a dual function, on the one hand they are there to offer support and advice to the facilitators, particularly to the novice facilitators, but they also ensure the quality of the programme. They observe sessions and provide feedback to facilitators and also to Soliya on the progress of the groups and their facilitators and indicate any areas of concern. This new identity offered me further perspectives from which to understand the Soliya Connect Program: on the macrolevel I gained insights as regards the structure of Soliya and its workings, and on a meso-level I was able to observe interactions across different groups, gain an understanding of the heterogeneity of groups and their interactions, but also the way the facilitators influenced these different groups' interactions.

These situated identities of mine within the Soliya Connect Program are illustrated below in Figure 4.1. The identities are not mutually exclusive, however. I have continued to be a Soliya professor while I trained and became a facilitator and coach, though I have never had my own students in the groups I facilitate. At the time of writing, I have my sixteenth cohort of students participating in the Connect Program.

Figure 4.1. Progression of my situated identities in relation to Soliya

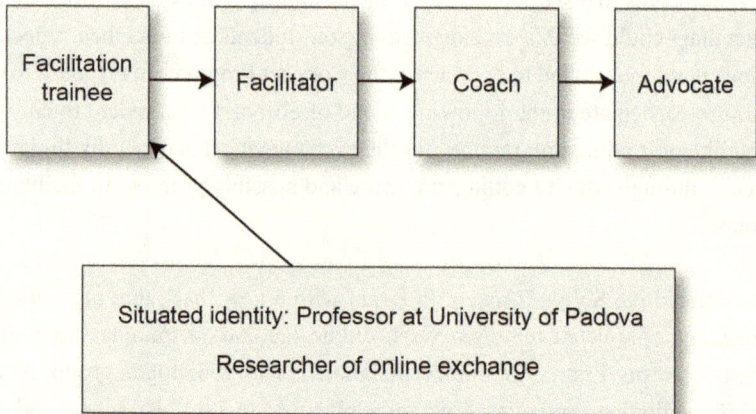

Through these various levels of engagement, and also due to my research interest in Virtual Exchange, I have had contact with many members of Soliya staff and have engaged considerably with the 'Soliya Community'. Staff have organised events such as webinars with members of the board, facilitators, and alumni. Through these activities and Soliya's interest in developing their network and working in Europe, I became further engaged in Soliya's advocacy work. Soliya joined forces with other American virtual exchange providers (Global Nomads Group, iEARN) in the Virtual Exchange Coalition[2] and concentrated their activities on gaining further recognition for the field of virtual exchange in general. I have also become involved in this activity to a certain degree, and was invited to meetings of the coalition with various stakeholders in Europe. My situated identity in these contexts was that of a European academic with experience of and research carried out on virtual exchange.

In the paragraphs above I have outlined the reasons that led me to Soliya, and also how my insider status has given me the opportunity of getting to know the

_____

2. http://virtualexchangecoalition.org

context of my study from a diversity of perspectives. This was important to specify because in ethnographic studies it is essential for the researcher to state 'where they are coming from', as the subjectivities of the researcher inevitably influence the studies they carry out. The different experiences of encounter and dialogue that I have had and continue to have through this community have offered me different ways of thinking and knowing and have led to self-reflection and learning experiences which continue beyond the confines of this study. At the same time, I am completely independent from Soliya, I work as a university researcher and seek to engage critically with the objects of my studies.

4.3. Data for this study: the dialogue group

As mentioned above, a key component of the Soliya Connect Program design is the dialogue groups. In every iteration of the Soliya Connect Program, students from partner universities are divided into small groups of eight to ten, with an equal distribution of students from 'Western societies' and 'predominantly Muslim societies' and with an equal balance in terms of gender as far as possible. The facilitators are also preferably from these two broad groups. It is clearly very difficult for Soliya to create every dialogue group to these specifications as they work under many constraints (for instance time zones, number of participants from different classes, local timetables, etc.), but this is the aim.

A group dynamic is expected to emerge through the exchange which allows participants to begin exploring different perspectives on what are often seen as controversial issues. According to the Soliya training materials (Soliya, 2010), there are several predictable stages in the group process. It starts with groups showing extreme politeness, not highlighting difference and carefully choosing their words. Groups then go into a more conflictual phase where various levels of disagreement may be reached and there can be intense emotion and lack of empathy for others. This is generally followed by a phase of frustration with the communication patterns (e.g. conversations going in circles) and then participants attempt to understand one another's perspectives. They also begin to explain their points of view in a way that individuals on 'the other side' can hear. According to this model, when groups have been working effectively in stage three for a while they feel they can spread what they have learnt to the broader community and may also think about how they can make an impact together, as a group. Clearly not all groups are expected to reach this final phase, nor is the group process linear. Every group is unique and dynamics within each group differ in every encounter. Nonetheless, having an understanding of group processes is expected to support facilitators in performing their institutional roles (Soliya, 2010).

The dialogue group whose interactions are object of this study 'met' in Soliya's 'main meeting room' over a period of seven weeks. I consider this online meeting room with this group of people a *situated context,* where participants have access to one another and a glimpse into one another's local physical surroundings through the small webcam picture. This context becomes a space in itself, with a culture and norms of behaviour of its own which, however, are influenced by a multiplicity of factors: the curriculum described above and the ideals of its developers who in turn have been influenced by the broader, socio-political context (see Chapter 5 for a more in-depth analysis of the situated context); the technology and its 'affordances' for communication (see Chapter 6 for a discussion of this from the perspective of the mediation principle); the individual participants and what they bring to the space which is influenced by aspects of what Blommaert (1991) – drawing on Bourdieu (1990) – would describe as their 'ethnic habitus' and aspects of their local contexts on a multiplicity of levels. However, it is within the context of and in relation to the group that participants' identities emerge, through their interactions across communication modes, as they position themselves and make relevant different aspects of their own and others' transportable identities.

It is also important to situate this group's discussions in the historic time in which they occurred, that is in the midst of the so-called 'Arab Spring', or the 'revolutions' which took place in much of the Southern Mediterranean in 2011. Events began[3] in Tunisia on the 17th of December 2010 after the self-immolation

---

3. Though clearly there were situations and events prior to these which laid the ground for the revolutions.

of Mohamed Bouazizi in Sidi Bouzid, and led to the ousting of Zine El Abidine Ben Ali in January 2011, who fled to Saudi Arabia after 23 years in power. The first day of occupation of Tahrir Square in Cairo was the 25th of January 2011, which marked the beginning of the Egyptian revolution that saw the ousting of Hosni Mubarak on the 11th of February 2011. The dialogue sessions began in March 2011.

In the dialogue group under study, there were two facilitators who had recently finished their training. Jessica was the 'Western' facilitator and Ranà, from the 'predominantly Muslim society', was a speaker of Arabic as well as English. There were ten participants: four male and six female, three from 'Western societies' and seven from 'predominantly Muslim societies'.

I have deliberately decided not to include a table listing participants' gender, countries of residence and disciplinary backgrounds as from an interaction-centred perspective, these become relevant only as and when the interactants themselves make them so. What this study sought to do was to explore why and how identities were oriented to by participants, and in what ways this influenced interaction, participation, and power dynamics.

Section 2.

Applying the framework

Exploring the situated context

In the theoretical framework, the first principle for the study of identity in interaction is the 'situatedness' principle, which highlights the fact that all identity work takes place in a situated context. The research questions I seek to answer in this chapter are:

- What identity positionings does the situated context of Soliya offer participants?

- What factors influence these positionings?

I ask these questions not because these are the only identity positionings available to the participants, nor do I wish to imply that they remain static, essentialised identities – but rather to acknowledge that they *may* have an influence on the interactions that take place within that site.

In order to answer these questions, I adopt the concept of 'epistechnical system' (Williamson, 2013). Developed in the field of educational technology, the term refers to the fusion and binding of technology and knowledge in curricular configurations. Williamson (2013) observes that like all technological and educational systems, epistechnical systems are *socially shaped* and *socially shaping,* that is they are not neutral, but rather "socially constructed and historically contingent" (p. 40), intentionally designed products which serve to influence and shape thought and action.

The Soliya Connect Program can be considered as an epistechnical system for it explicitly aims to influence thought and action. Adopting this lens allows me to identify the factors which influence the available identity positionings, and also to embrace a critical understanding of the context.

Williamson's (2013) framework is a critical approach to the study of educational technology. Published in the volume the *Politics of Education and Technology*, he offers a method which facilitates interpretation on different levels. In order to understand educational technology in relation to its connections to a larger society, he argues that political and sociological issues need to be introduced into the narrative. Selwyn and Facer (2013) argue that educational technology should be seen as a site of negotiation and struggle between different actors, which include the designers and developers of new tools and curricula, consultants, funders and advocates, as well as those whom the educational projects are addressing, their families and communities. It needs to be explored on a 'macro' level of social structure of society as well as the microlevel of the individual and the learning context.

In attempting to take a critical stance, I thus look at the politics embodied in the epistechnical system I am studying, the Soliya Connect Program, by asking what authority and expertise has contributed to its design? "What politics and values and what kinds of prospective identities, actions, and forms of 'learning' are to be shaped and sculpted" (Williamson, 2013, p. 40) through this system? I will seek to answer these questions first of all by analysing the website and documentation produced and published by Soliya in order to offer a rich description of the organisation behind the programme and its development, and seek to identify contradictions and tensions inherent in the programme.

5.1. Soliya as an epistechnical system

The Soliya Connect Program can be considered as an epistechnical system because it seeks to transform individuals, not by making them subscribe to a particular point of view, but by offering them "the opportunity to genuinely re-examine and analyse pre-existing opinions and beliefs in a space in which transformation and reconsideration of existing views is possible" (Soliya, 2010, p. 6). The declared aim is to empower participants and develop their sense of responsibility in contributing to making a more positive relationship between 'Western societies' and 'predominantly Muslim societies' by seeking to foster greater understanding for other perspectives on issues which are seen to be divisive, and which education has often chosen to ignore. At the same time, the project also claims to offer participants the possibility to develop '21st century skills', including cross-cultural communication, media literacy, and critical thinking (see Figure 5.1 below).

Figure 5.1. Screenshot of Soliya website: what we do[1]

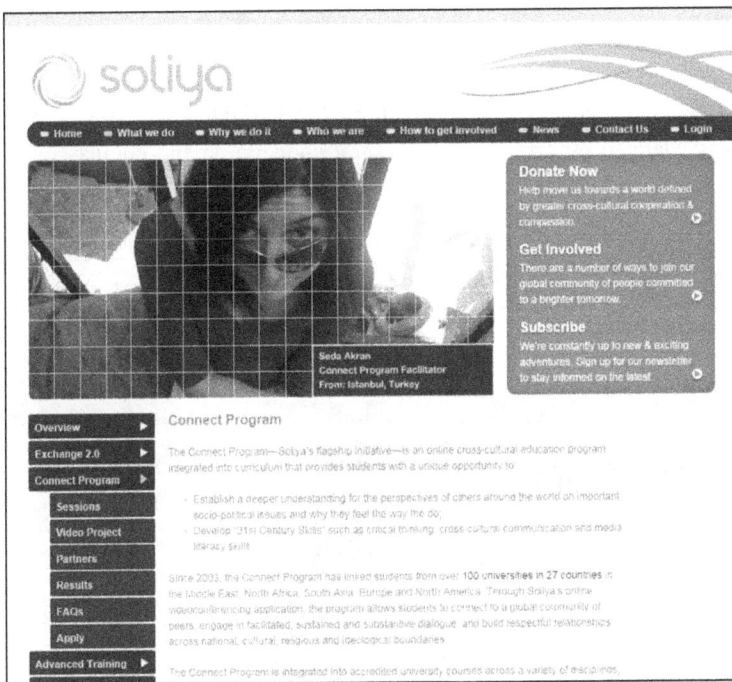

Looking at 'Who we are' on Soliya's website, the organisation defines itself as :

> "a dynamic network of staff, university partners and students, volunteer facilitators, trainers and coaches, Soliya Fellows and civil society partners, along with a dedicated Board of Directors, advisors and funders.

---

1. The website has been updated since the study was carried out. Reproduced with kind permissions from © Soliya.

Our team represents thought leaders, experienced practitioners and emerging young activists in the fields of new media and technology, social entrepreneurship, conflict resolution, advocacy and international affairs".

The website has a series of slides with large photos of individuals which appear on the left hand side – changing to reflect a young, culturally diverse community, located in a range of locations, some of them holding media tools such as video cameras. This imagery and text reinforce its definition of itself as a diverse, global community (the name, role and location of each person appears with their photo) engaged in adventure and "committed to a brighter tomorrow" in a world which is "defined by greater cross-cultural cooperation and compassion" (see Figure 5.2).

Figure 5.2. Soliya website: who we are[2]

---

2. Reproduced with kind permissions from © Soliya.

The buttons on the right hand side of the page (Donate Now, Get Involved, Subscribe) also serve to identify Soliya[3] as a non-profit organisation which seeks donations from funding bodies and the involvement and generation of a community or network of people who subscribe to the activities and ideals of Soliya.

On the website, there is no specification of the geographical location of Soliya as an organisation. It is presented very much as a **network** of people, with different levels of involvement and some form of hierarchy. Soliya has a board of directors and staff members, who are split into an executive team, and staff members. Photos and bios of board and staff members are present on the site, and from some of the biographies it is possible to infer where they are located, some in the US or Egypt, but not all. The staff team represents a diversity of backgrounds and experiences, and many members with experience of living and/ or studying abroad. Soliya's network members are the University partners, now listing over 100 across much of the world, and the Soliya Network of alumni; people who participated in Soliya as part of their university studies and some of whom have continued to collaborate as volunteer facilitators. The Soliya Connect Program can be seen to embody what Williamson (2013) defines as "networked cosmopolitanism", that is, "a way of thinking about the future that is infused with normative ideas about the cosmopolitan potential of networks" which blends cosmopolitan principles of autonomy and self-responsibility with network notions of connectivity "to motivate a particular style of belonging in the (imagined) future of a globalised society" (p. 43).

5.2. Problems and solutions

The development of an epistechnical system entails the construction of an 'imagined future' for young people (Williamson, 2013, p.43), and curriculum developers construct consensus and legitimacy by fashioning particular

---

3. The name Soliya, as reported on the website, "integrates the Latin word for sun, sol, and an ancient Arabic word for light, iya (ﻟﻴﺎ). The word 'iya' is rare, but can be found in the Mu'allaqat, or The Hanging Poems, a collection of renowned pre-Islamic poems that hang on the Ka'aba. The name reflects our aim to bridge divides and shed light on cultural differences that too often seem inevitable and intractable".

problems to which they propose a solution. The main problem the Soliya developers identify is the negative approach to difference which characterises the relationship between 'Western' and 'predominantly Muslim societies' and the widespread perception of an inevitable 'clash of civilizations', which responses to 9/11 seemed to invoke. As they write on their website:

> "We believe that the fundamental challenge is to shift the dominant paradigm for how our societies resolve differences from an approach defined by confrontation & coercion to one defined by cooperation & compassion. This need is particularly acute in relations between Western and predominantly Muslim societies. Hundreds of thousands of people have been killed and trillions of dollars spent since the turn of the century in what many see as an inevitable 'Clash of Civilizations'"[4].

Similar concerns have also been recognised in the field of foreign language education, with a wide range of publications on the role of language in the public sphere and foreign language teaching since 9/11. For example, from the US perspective, Heidi Byrnes (2004) wrote:

> "A post 9/11 world affords the language profession a much-needed opportunity to revise its notions of the role of language in the public sphere. For no cultural and linguistic world have the events of 9/11 and its aftermath affected views of 'the other' more dramatically than for the Arabic speaking world, often lumped together with the Islamic world, often lumped together with uncivilized societies and terrorism" (p. 267).

A further problem Soliya identifies is that 'traditional' education and media are not addressing the problem effectively. The problem with the media has been identified in research carried out on stereotyping, according to which inaccurate beliefs of media stereotypes of particular groups are reinforced in viewers that have had little direct contact with these groups (see Argo, Idriss, & Fancy,

---

4. The original text and webpage can no longer be found.

2009)[5]. Further research has found that emotion plays a more central role in forming our judgements, worldviews, and values than cognitive reasoning. The Soliya website states that media coverage is serving to polarise groups rather than bring them together, while social media have given individuals the power to influence increasing numbers of people. That is, 'influencers' can have expansively destructive impacts, for example the pastor in Florida who burnt the Quran in 2011, which led to protests in Afghanistan where 20 people were killed[6] or more recently ISIS strategists who adeptly used social media to recruit fighters[7]. In face of this, Soliya seeks to create a generation of 'influencers' who will have a positive impact[8], as I will discuss in the following section.

5.3. Transportable and imagined identities

As the Soliya Connect Program is based on theories of conflict transformation and intergroup relations, it makes relevant the transportable identity categories of the broad social groups involved in this 'conflict': 'Western societies' and 'predominantly Muslim societies'[9]. This framing can be seen to represent one of the tensions of this curriculum, as in order to address problematic intergroup relations, it is necessary to define the groups. The use of such broad social group labels is problematic as it indexes homogeneity and ignores the political, religious, economic, social, and demographic heterogeneity within these groups. It is also strategic, for problematising these labels and the language used to talk about the 'other' is part of the Soliya Connect Program activities. One of the questions I explore in the following chapters is whether more heterogeneous identities emerge within the interactions of the dialogue group (as indeed the programme intends) or if the participants stick to these broad social group labels.

---

5. A link to this study is published on their website

6. http://www.independent.co.uk/news/world/americas/burning-the-koran-is-not-radical-says-controversial-american-pastor-terry-jones-as-he-searches-for-9985986.html

7. https://www.wired.com/2016/03/isis-winning-social-media-war-heres-beat/

8. The original text and webpage can no longer be found.

9. Soliya counterposes 'Western societies', using a broad geographic term, with 'predominantly Muslim societies', a term which defines a group on the basis of religion rather than geography, at times also using the phrase 'predominantly Arab and/or Muslim societies'.

As mentioned in the theoretical framework, the notion of imagined identities is also a key construct in language learning. The notion of imagination as suggested by Anderson (1991) and developed by Wenger (1998) as regards communities of practice has been adopted by Norton (2000/2013), who argues that it is a way for learners to appropriate meanings and create new identities, transcending their immediate environment. Language learners may invest in those who provide them with access to their imagined communities (Pavlenko & Norton, 2007), but it is not just language learning contexts, for all types of educational environments, from the classroom to the institution (Kanno, 2003), the offline to the online, the formal to the non-formal, have visions for their students' futures.

The imagined future that Soliya constructs in its narrative is one of "greater peace and prosperity for the next generation", as reported on their website[10]. In their view, this can be achieved by changing how societies approach difference, for instance by preparing a generation of 'influencers', who can address emerging tensions and create a positive interdependence capable of addressing future challenges. The solution they propose to the problem of intergroup relations is a model of education and media literacy which can create this new generation who are committed to "cooperative and compassionate approaches to difference"[11]. The institutionally defined *imagined identity* is thus that of an 'influencer', somebody who can use the networking power of new media technologies to change societies. Becoming involved with Soliya means joining "a global community of people committed to a brighter tomorrow" (website: Get Involved tab) and is a way into this global network, which is represented visually on the Soliya website through the gallery of photos of individuals belonging to the Soliya community as seen in Figure 5.2 above. Whether this imagined identity is shared or indexed by the participants themselves through their interactions shall also be explored in this study.

The prospective view offered by Soliya, its self-definition as a network, echoes many characteristics of the modern identity evoked in Williamson's (2013)

---

10. The original text and webpage can no longer be found.

11. The original text and webpage can no longer be found.

'networked cosmopolitanism', which is "embodied in talk about autonomy, self-responsibility, respect for diversity and difference, and participation and collaboration in communities, with a focus on the creation of a 'good' or 'ethical' future" (p. 46). What we identify as a 'good' future needs defining though.

Martha Nussbaum (1996), the well-known American philosopher and theorist of global justice, defined cosmopolitanism as offering one's principal loyalty "to the moral community made up by the humanity of all beings" (p. 7). Camicia and Franklin (2010) build on her definition and identify two strands of cosmopolitan discourse, which communicate two different visions for community. The first, 'neoliberal cosmopolitanism', defines global citizens as a community of self-starting entrepreneurs who function in terms of a market rationale. The second, 'democratic cosmopolitanism', defines global citizens as a community of diverse individuals with a mindset oriented towards cultural representation, human rights, and social justice.

We find traces of both discourses in Soliya's imagined future of 'greater peace and prosperity' described above. These discourses also appear in the goals of the Soliya curriculum, as defined on their website[12]. The first set of goals specified on the website are in line with this form of democratic cosmopolitanism which is concerned with cultural representation:

> "Establish a deeper understanding for the perspectives of others around the world on important socio-political issues and why they feel the way they do".

The second set of goals, with an emphasis on skills, hints at the neoliberal discourse which has permeated education policy and focusses on skills-sets which are required for the 21st century workplace:

> "Develop '21st century skills' such as critical thinking, cross-cultural communication and media literacy skills".

---

12. The original text and webpage can no longer be found.

As Rose (2009) writes, the philosophy behind 21st century skills is an economic one, and the civic, social, and ethical reasons for developing 'cross-cultural communication skills' and 'critical thinking' are lost sight of, as they are generally expressed in terms of workplace effectiveness (as in the Partnership for 21st Century Skills[13]). In Chapter 8, I explore if the participants evoke either of these 'networked cosmopolitan' identities as their imagined identities in their interactions.

5.4. Tensions and contradictions in the Soliya Connect Program

5.4.1. Western aims and model?

The goals of the Connect Program may resonate well with educators who believe that they should aim to challenge stereotypes and foster intercultural awareness and understanding in learners, who see their role not as transmitting knowledge but rather sowing the seeds of doubt in students to enable them to become critical thinkers. Yet do these goals reflect only the 'Western' educational ideals of the programme's developers, and is there a risk that these are imposed on Soliya's partners in education?

Maha Bali (2013), whose PhD thesis explores critical thinking in an American liberal arts university in Egypt – and which looks at the Soliya Connect Program as one of several projects adopted to enhance this, has addressed this issue. Critical thinking, as pointed out by Bali (2013, p. 28), is considered by many to be a Western-influenced educational ideal which opposes Arab and Muslim cultural values (Cook, 1999). For example, critical thinking encourages people to accommodate various perspectives and see several truths as equally viable, whilst Islam is tolerant of different perspectives but does not consider them all to be equally valid, and claims a single universal truth (Cook, 1999). However, she points out that other scholars (Nurullah, 2006; Said, 2004) have contrasted

---

13. http://www.p21.org/

this view of Islam, arguing that the concept of 'ijtihad' (which applies critical and creative thinking to new situations in Islamic law) is fundamental in interpreting Islam and applying Islamic law (sharia), and can result in multiple divergent but equally valid interpretations (Bali, 2013, pp. 28-29). It has been argued that today there is a lack of critical thinking in Islamic scholars and their followers, Bali (2013) continues, and that this process of 'ijtihad' has given way to 'taqlid' (or blind emulation), despite encouragement for critical reflection and creative thinking in the Quran and Sunnah (Nurullah, 2006). I am in no position to make judgements on this issue for it goes well beyond the aims of this thesis. Furthermore, I am a 'Western' scholar working in Europe with very limited knowledge of Islam. However, I would agree with Bali who points out that critical thinking is not necessarily alive and kicking across the United States or in Europe[14].

A further issue is the willingness and ability of participants to engage in this dialogic type of communication. Bali (2014) argues that the dialogic model privileges students who are familiar with interactive classrooms, such as Western students. Whilst this may be the case for students from some Western, Anglophone contexts, I would argue that many European students in higher education are not familiar with interactive, dialogic classes, for the predominant pedagogic model remains the transmission of knowledge through lectures (European Commission, 2013).

5.4.2. The language issue

As is clear from the information provided thus far, the Soliya Connect Program was not developed as an English language programme, but it has been adopted in advanced English language courses in various institutes in Europe (including my own context, the University of Padova, Italy) and the Middle East. The rationale for this is that it is a form of experiential learning which integrates content and language use. As well as being an opportunity for developing their English language, and also acquiring knowledge about issues which affect

---

14. https://www.theguardian.com/teacher-network/2012/sep/12/critical-thinking-overlooked-in-secondary-education

the relationship between 'Western societies' and the 'predominantly Muslim societies', the Soliya Connect Program allows participants to develop new online literacies (Guth & Helm, 2010), such as communicating in synchronous online video, using text and audio chat simultaneously, multi-tasking, and video production skills.

However, the fact that English is the language of communication between participants means that about half of the participants are expressing themselves in their second, possibly third, fourth (or more) language, on controversial and emotional issues. This creates power inequalities and introduces issues of cultural and linguistic capital, as Bali (2013, 2014) argues, for the American participants who are already in many respects the 'dominant' side. Also, the participants with better English and more exposure to the American culture find it easier to have a conversation. While having an Arabic-speaking facilitator can help, when the Arabic facilitators themselves are less fluent in English the situation can be exacerbated, Bali (2013) maintains. The choice of English can be seen to reflect a global need for a shared language in order for intercultural dialogue to take place, but this creates inequalities in power relations:

> "We [the minorities] and you [the dominant] do not talk the same language. When we talk to you we use your language: the language of your experience and of your theories. We try to use it to communicate our world of experience. But since your language and your theories are inadequate in expressing our experiences, we only succeed in communicating our experience of exclusion. We cannot talk to you in our language because you do not understand it" (Lugones & Spelman, 1983, p. 575, quoted in Bali & Sharma, 2014, n.p.).

Soliya has acknowledged this to a certain extent in the facilitation training by advising facilitators to support those who are not so fluent in English by summarising conversations in text chat, and addressing the language issue with some activities which are intended to raise awareness of the language issue.

This again is a tension and contradiction in Soliya. Alternative possibilities could be making Arabic the main language of the programme, and having the support of translators. This, however, clashes with the 'hinted at' neoliberal discourse and 'soft sell' of the Soliya Connect Program. Furthermore, as the programme has been increasing, the opportunity to use and improve their English is a motivation for many of the students in the 'predominantly Muslim world' to participate in Soliya Connect Program, as witnessed by the number of students in predominantly Muslim countries taking part in the Soliya Connect Program as part of their English courses[15].

---

15. Information received from Soliya about established partnerships.

Mediated identities

"The implication for cultures-of-use is to expand our thinking to include the ontological possibility that it is not only humans who act on, with, and through technologies, but that technologies may also be acting on, with, and through us" (Thorne, 2016, p. 189).

In the previous chapter, I analysed the situated context of Soliya through its website, which represents its exterior public image that serves to promote and disseminate the project. Through this I showed how Soliya is intentionally designed to offer possibilities for doing 'identity work' on different levels, both in terms of situated identities (facilitators and participants) and transportable identities – with reference being made in particular to the identity categories of 'Westerner', 'Muslim' and 'non-Muslim', for these are the identities which the framing of the programme focusses on, and also imagined identities. Before exploring how participants orient to these situated and transportable identities through indexicality and relationality in Chapters 7 and 8, I am going to explore the affordances and constraints of the mediating technologies available for doing identity work in the situated context of this study.

In this chapter, I describe the closed areas of Soliya, that is the areas that only registered participants, alumni, and Soliya staff and facilitators have access to. There are two main components of this space, the Soliya community area with individual blogs for each participant and the meeting rooms where the participants meet for their weekly synchronous dialogue sessions. This chapter will provide an overview of the affordances and constraints of the mediating tools in these two spaces, with examples of how participants' discourse and situated and/or transportable identities emerged first of all through asynchronous text and images in the blog, and then through synchronous text, video, and audio interactions in the meeting room. Like all communication

(Kern, 2015), the communication in these online spaces is multimodal, but for the purpose of analysis in this chapter I initially consider each mode separately, as advised by researchers on multimodality (Bezemer & Jewitt, 2010).

6.1. The mediation principle

"The medium matters" (Kern, 2014, p. 341).

As explained in the theoretical framework (Chapter 3), the 'mediation principle' acknowledges the fact that in online environments, the technologies we use have a mediating effect on the interaction, the affordances, and constraints of the tools we use, and contribute to the meaning making process and also to the process of identity construction. The act of mediation thus does not merely facilitate, or complicate, processes, but it radically transforms them (Kern, 2014).

Mediating tools are not neutral and they do not simply 'exist', they are designed with specific purposes and aims which are reflected in the tools themselves. For example, Twitter was designed as an SMS-based communications platform to be used by friends for status updates[1], hence the limit of 140 characters, as this was the limit that mobile carriers imposed. Even though it subsequently moved to a web platform, the character limit remained, 'as a creative constraint', according to the developers. As Twitter's user base grew, they began to create new jargon and different ways of using the service, for example using the @ symbol to identify other users, or hashtags # to group messages and content into categories so users can more easily find relevant content. This example serves to illustrate how interactants can exercise agency as they use online tools. The relationship between tools and their users is, to a certain degree, reciprocal. This is why online interaction and identity construction should not be studied without a consideration of the tools being used to mediate the interaction.

---

1. http://twitter.about.com/od/Twitter-Basics/a/The-Real-History-Of-Twitter-In-Brief.htm

Much of the early work around online identities focussed on the affordances that the anonymity of computer-mediated communication – a term which still now is often used to refer to text-only communication – for identity construction. Whilst the notions of identity construction and anonymity might appear to be complete opposites, in text-based computer-mediated communication, anonymity can actually play an important role in how identity is constructed, which would be much more difficult in face to face situations.

Interaction through webcams does not allow for the anonymity that text-based computer-mediated communication offers participants, but it is quite different from face to face communication in a physical space in many respects. Malinowski and Kramsch (2014) have called into question the authenticity of online interaction and in particular the ability of synchronous computer mediated communication and video-conferencing technology "to replicate offline, embodied interaction" (p. 4). I would argue, however, that in using these technologies for online interaction, the aim should not be to replicate face to face interaction, but rather to learn to communicate effectively and construct and negotiate identity positions in these environments which constitute authentic contexts in their own right (Develotte, Guichon, & Vincent, 2010). In much the same way as educators have gradually come to recognise text-based computer-mediated communication as a "high stakes, high frequency context for all manner of professional, academic and social activity" (Thorne, Black, & Sykes, 2009, p. 803), so they soon will for audio and video-mediated communication.

Text-based computer-mediated communication in its diverse forms constitutes many different genres of written communication, which continue to use historically rooted text conventions and may share some characteristics of 'traditional' genres, but also develop their own distinct features. The same will soon be the case for audio-video-text mediated communication, which is increasingly being used in our networked lives. There are already many different audio-video conferencing tools, with a range of additional modes of communication: text chat, emojis, turn taking tools (such as the hand icon which can be clicked to indicate the desire to take the floor), shared whiteboards, shared images, presentation displays, and the list goes on. There are also many possible configurations of participants (e.g. one to one, one to many, many to many) and different 'genres' of video-conference ranging from monologic lectures with text-based questions to board meetings, from medical consultations to transglobal political activist meetings to cite just a few. These online situated contexts and genres may share some features with their face to face equivalents but they will also differ considerably. In all of these online (and offline) sites there are both situated identities established by the 'institutional' context, but there are also individuals who may make relevant other aspects of their identities as the interaction unfolds, using the available meaning-making resources. The degree of agency they can have over their identity construction and negotiation depends in part on their understanding and mastery of the mediating tools available to them – which include language and also the technologies.

Malinowski and Kramsch (2014) look in particular at the dimensions of representation, time, and space in desktop videoconferencing and language learning contexts. They identify two aspects of synchronous computer mediated communication which are particularly salient in terms of representation as experienced by online language learners: framing and segmentation. Our experience of space, time, and the 'real' is moved to the plane of representation which we see through the 'window' of the computer screen, which frames or delimits what we – and others – see. Our sense of hearing is 'segmented' through earphones or speakers, and voices sometimes echo back and can have a disorienting effect. As regards time, through video-conferencing participants often experience 'latency', that is the time lag between the real time performance of an action and its representation on the screen, as well as gaps between sound and images, with interactants' faces sometimes 'freezing'.

The spaces which users can orient their attention to are multiple and include the online or virtual space in which the interaction takes place, the physical space surrounding the computer, or the 'hors-champ' (Guichon & Wigham, 2016), the 'champ', which is the screen space (which can make available several different online spaces in different windows), and other 'places' or geographic sites that interactants can refer to. This can make it difficult to disambiguate the gestures, expressions, and body language that are seen through the video cameras during conversation. Furthermore, eye contact can be a problem as interlocutors must choose to look either at the partners' on screen representation or at the camera (to feign direct eye contact). These "disjunctures in the flow of space and time profoundly affect the possibilities for heteroglossic language learning" (Malinowski & Kramsch, 2014, p. 6) in synchronous, multimodal telecollaboration, for they are seen to detract interactants' attention from engagement in deeper negotiation of social and cultural meanings.

However, for some researchers, the multimodal (visual, audio, and textual) nature of such environments, in spite of its limitations, is regarded as beneficial to negotiation of meaning (see Chun & Plass, 2000). Furthermore, the impact of video on building a learning community, increasing confidence, and reducing isolation is largely recognised in the literature (see Guichon & Wigham, 2016; Hampel & Hauck, 2006; Hampel & Stickler, 2012), particularly for learners who are physically isolated from one another, and for whom video is perceived as being even more crucial in reducing the impact of the distance.

The way participants orient to modes can be an important part of their identity construction. Lamy (2012), for instance, found that in multimodal contexts participants can specialise particular conversational aims to different spaces on the screen or choose modes, and that the different modes used can thus reflect different images of the same person. In Lamy's study, a content analysis of input of participants in a multimodal conversation showed that one participant's input through the spoken channel was mainly asking for others' opinions, whilst all text-chat inputs were language accuracy checks. This led to the hypothesis that face-saving issues were involved as regards self-representation, with the participant giving an image of himself as a confident English speaker in the audio mode, whilst using the text chat for more face-threatening activities such as asking for help with English forms. These findings are in line with Blake (2000), who found that learners chose the less face-threatening text chat over the voice chat to request help from the tutor.

As briefly outlined in Chapter 2, the emergence and phenomenal success of social networking sites have somewhat changed the dynamics and attitudes towards anonymity because their main aim is for users to curate their identities and their personal, social, and/or professional networks[2]. Construction and negotiation of identities online has become a rich area of research and much of the recent work has focussed on the affordances of social networking sites and multimodal media used for engaging in 'identity work' (boyd, 2006; Buckingham, 2008). The profile page in particular is held to be key to the dynamic of interaction and identity construction in online communities (Harrison & Thomas, 2009), though the degree of authenticity of these profiles has been found to vary (boyd, 2008). Key aspects of self-presentation on social network profiles are visual self portrayals, through photos or avatars, and the articulation of friendship links (boyd & Ellison, 2007, p. 10).

The literature from the field of language learning and technology as regards online identities mainly regards identity construction in public sites and networks such as online discussion forums (Hanna & de Nooy, 2009), social networking sites (Chen, 2013; Harrison & Thomas, 2009; Lam, 2000, 2006; Reinhardt & Chen, 2013), and gaming and fanfiction spaces (Sauro, 2014; Thorne, Sauro, & Smith, 2015). Much less work has been carried out in the educational contexts of online intercultural exchange projects which generally take place in closed, private spaces such as institutional platforms. These two different types of spaces, the public versus the private, the recreational versus the educational, have often been presented as a dichotomy, but this is an over-simplification. There are several projects which can be seen to lie at the interstices of the formal and informal sphere (Thorne, Sauro, & Smith, 2015), and Soliya could be seen as one of these.

6.2. Mediation and multimodality

The assumption underlying my discussion and analysis of identity work through technology-mediated interaction is that all interaction is multimodal (Kern, 2015, p. 223), even in face to face contexts. Technologies have simply added

---

2. This is not to say, however, that trolling is not also a phenomenon on social networks.

new modalities and channels of communication and multiplied the ways in which these can be combined as we engage in meaning making. Technologies can facilitate or favour different kinds of meaning making and identity work, they can also constrain them through the design of the tools themselves and the differential access to the means of production and reception of these meanings (Kress & van Leeuwen, 1996).

I will first offer some clarifications as regards the terminology I will be using since the concept of multimodality has been applied in different disciplinary areas. Since this study lies within the area of language learning and technology, I have chosen to adopt the terminology used in this field, as recently defined by Guichon and Cohen (2016), "*Multimodality* makes sensory information accessible in diverse semiotic modes and offers the opportunity to produce, comprehend and exchange information simultaneously through different channels" (p. 510). *Mode*, then, defines the type of semiotic representation (in this study I look at textual, oral, and visual) used to present information. *Media* (e.g. a video clip, or a conversation in video conferencing) are the technological means of inscription and production that shape the ways a message is conveyed and accessed. These can be static, dynamic, or interactive.

In Table 6.1, which is adapted from Guichon and Cohen (2016), I summarise the nature and temporality of the different media and the semiotic modes of the two environments I explore in this chapter: the Soliya community area with asynchronous blogs and the meeting rooms for synchronous audio-video sessions.

Table 6.1. Media and modes in this project

Medium	Temporality of the medium	Nature of the medium	Semiotic modes
Individual blog in the Soliya community area	Asynchronous	Static	Textual (written blog posts) and visual (photographs)
Video-conferencing meeting room for two hour synchronous sessions	Synchronous	Interactive	Textual (text chat), oral (interlocutors' voices), visual (webcam image of interlocutors)

6.3. The Soliya community area: asynchronous identities

My starting point of analysis in this chapter will be the Soliya Community area, since this is the first space that participants come into contact with when they have registered for the programme. It is also where they first have to begin to 'construct' their identities, as upon registering for the project participants are asked to complete their personal blog.

6.3.1. Affordances of the blogs

The individual blog spaces include two key components for online identity formation (Gonzales & Hancock, 2008), that is the presentation of demographic information (name, birthday, photo, and so forth), and the potential for an audience. The most immediate audience here is their Soliya dialogue group (which consists of the ten people who will be interacting together over the seven week period) as the blogs are gathered together under a tab 'My Group' for all the group members to see. However, the whole Soliya community, which consists of all present and past Soliya participants and facilitators, is potentially able to see their blog posts.

The blog offers opportunities for identity construction in both visual and textual modes for writing on the blog, for instance, participants can post small thumbnail photos of themselves (which most members of the community do). However not all members of the Soliya group in this study have done so.

The first blog post that participants are asked to write has five informal questions they can choose to answer. The questions are as follows:

- Where are you from? What is it like there?

- How do you spend your time? What do you enjoy doing most?

- What do you want to be doing in ten years? Where do you want to live?

- If you were throwing a dinner party and could invite any four people in the world, who would you invite and why?

- Why did you decide to participate in this programme?

In terms of identity construction, these questions offer the participants several possibilities – they can choose to make relevant aspects of their transportable identities, such as their nationality/ies, but also other aspects which are related to their interests, ambitions, and also their motivations for taking part in this programme (which as we see later in the synchronous sessions contributes to the authenticity of their situated identity as a 'Soliya participant'). Question 3 asks what they want to be doing in ten years, offering them the possibility to think about, and also share their imagined identities with others. At the time they write this blog post the participants have not yet 'met' their fellow group members, this blog post can thus be seen as their first presentation of themselves to their fellow group members and to their 'imagined community'.

Responses to these questions from the members of the dialogue group varied in length and in terms of engagement with the questions, ranging from 'monosyllabic' responses to quite articulated responses to some of the questions which also allow the participants to give some insight into their personalities, for instance through humour.

It is worth noting that neither of the facilitators (Ranà and Jessica) have this information on their blogs, indeed neither of them published much information about themselves. This is in line with the situated identity of the facilitator – as somebody who is neutral and multipartial – and thus discloses little personal information about themselves.

6.3.2. Transportable identities

Participants orient to the first question about their place of origin in different ways, some explicitly indexing a strong sense of national identity and pride. Mohammed, for instance, writes "I'm from Egypt to me it's heaven on earth", and he uses the visual mode to reinforce the text; the photo of himself indexes his national identity; in the background of the picture is a pyramid with the colours of the Egyptian flag painted on it (Figure 6.1).

Figure 6.1. Mohammed's blog[3]

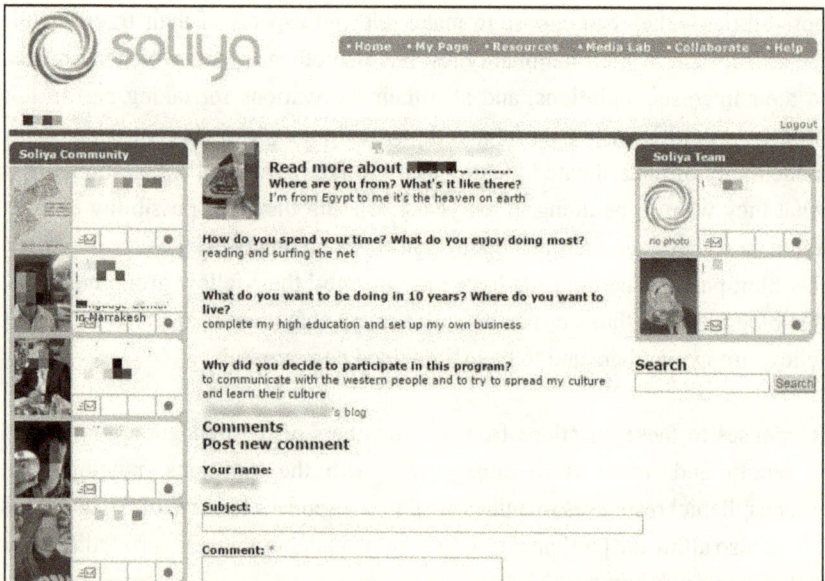

Fadela also indexes a strong pride in her place of origin as she writes "I am from Palestine, the PARADISE of this Planet!". The theme 'Palestine as Paradise' is a strong motif in Palestinian collective memory and has been recurrent in Palestinian folk culture and popular and nationalist discourse for over six decades, since the *Nakba* (the 'catastrophe') that the Palestinians experienced as a result of the 1947-1948 Arab-Israeli War over the possession of Palestine (Matar, 2011, p. 25). In the other posts she makes on her blog, Fadela indexes her Palestinian identity by mentioning the 'day of the land' March 30th (which commemorates a moment in 1976 when Palestinian citizens marched across

_____

3. Reproduced with kind permissions from © Soliya.

Galilee to protest Israel's evacuation, confiscation, and enclosure of their land). Her blog posts also mention other recurrent themes in collective Palestinian memory such as the martyrs, and prisoners in Israeli jails.

Alef makes relevant that his home town, Sidi Bouzid, "a small agrarian village in the south" of Tunisia was home of the Tunisian 'Jasmine revolution'. Sidi Bouzid is the town where the self-immolation of Mohamed Bouazizi occurred in December 2010, which led to massive protests and the ousting of president Ben Ali in January 2011. Alef thus makes relevant not only place but also time, a historical moment since the project started less than two months after the 'Jasmine revolution' began in Tunisia. We will see in the following chapters the extent to which these aspects of their transportable identities, which are indexed in this first presentation through the asynchronous blog mode, emerge in their synchronous interactions with the group.

As regards the other participants, Thamena and Doja also comment on their places of origin, Amman, the capital of Jordan ("a lovely city with simple people and nice weather"), and Jordan ("it's beautiful and nice"), but offering minimal information. Maawa, also from Jordan, does not make any additional comments as regards her origin.

Brendan specifies the town he is from in the U.S.A and says "It's fun, you just have to look around", and makes relevant his status as a full time student and also having a job. Jack and Deni both index their places of origin in the US as well as the location of their universities, which are not in their hometowns. None of the American participants index their American identity through visual symbols in their blog posts.

Participants make relevant other aspects of their transportable identities in their blog posts. Several make reference to music as something they enjoy and communities related to music that they are members of, for instance Deni who sings in an a cappella group, Jack who plays electric bass in a metal band, Alef who spends time listening to metal rock music, and Brendan who sees live music when he is not doing school work.

A couple of participants index their religion in their responses to Question 4 about who they would invite for dinner: Thamena says she would invite the prophet Muhammad "because I long to see him personally" – though she does not explicitly say she is a Muslim, and Jack says he would invite Jesus; "I'm a Christian, and even though I think God is everywhere, Jesus went through a lot and was the Son of God".

Mohammed and Thamena both make reference to their use of Internet as a hobby, indexing themselves as experienced Internet users. Interestingly, we see this to a certain degree reflected in their participation patterns in the online sessions – both are quite active – and in their text mode identities, particularly Thamena as we will see in the next section of this chapter.

6.3.3. Learners or users of English?

Several of the participants position themselves as English learners in their responses to the question asking why they decided to participate in the programme. They do not explicitly use the category of language learner, but Fadela, Thamena, Doha, and Maawa all used the verb 'to improve' their English/ language/speaking/communication in response to the question. Positioning themselves as learners or not expert speakers of English indexes a deficit view of their English competence and reflects the pervading categorisation that characterises foreign language education (Davies, 2003; Firth & Wagner, 1997; Jenkins, 2007; Rampton, 1990).

Several of the participants, however, made relevant their identity as users of English. Alef, for instance, in response to Question 2, reported that he had founded an English club at his college where he regularly meets other students for Drama/ Theater workshops, discussion, cinema, and in response to Question 3, he wrote "Ten years from now?! That's hard to answer, but most probable I'm gonna be teaching English somewhere in my country or in the Arab world. Still I'd like to live and work in the US". He thus positions himself as an active, competent, and enthusiastic user of English and familiar with informal language (use of gonna), with an interest in the US. Thamena, like Alef, also expresses a desire to go to the US (or UK) to study abroad, though specifies she wants to return to Jordan on finishing her studies, in response to Question 3. Her positioning thus shifts, for as well as a learner needing to improve, she also positions herself as a language user, not making reference specifically to English but saying that in her free time she sometimes translates and that she wants to be a professional translator in the future. Mohammed wrote that his reason for participating was "to communicate with the western people and try to spread my culture and learn their culture". He does not specifically mention the English language so he does not index 'learner' identity, but rather 'English user' identity, as it is through the mediation of English and the technology that he will be able to engage in this communication and achieve his aim.

6.3.4. Prospective identities

The blogs were where participants could invest in the 'prospective identity' that the Soliya Connect Program offers participants, for this is where they have the opportunity to engage with the broader Soliya Community as well as their own group members. Only three of the participants used their personal blog space to communicate after their initial introductory page: Alef, Fadela, and Mohammed. Alef's post was published online during the first week of the project and together with a photograph he writes about his experience volunteering in refugee camps on the border with Libya, indexing his active engagement with sociopolitical issues. This is an experience he was eager to talk about in the first dialogue session, as he made several references to it. This blog post had several comments over the following weeks, a couple from fellow group members, others from members of the Soliya community. However he did not publish any further posts on the blog.

Fadela also published three blog posts, all of which reflect her Palestinian identity. The first is a poem by Mahmoud Darwish, the Palestinian poet. The second is a picture of herself wearing a graduation outfit (which was actually a response to a request from one of the facilitators in the third dialogue session to post a picture of her graduation after she had told the group that she would be graduating). In the photo, her Palestinian identity is marked with *keffiyeh* over her shoulder. On the same day, she also made another post which relates to an issue she mentioned in the same dialogue session which is the 'day of the land in Palestine'. She makes reference to the resistance of the Palestinian people: "Today is the day of the land. Palestinians celebrate this day as a rebirth of their insistence to get Palestine free". There are several references to the situation of Palestine as a stolen land. She makes reference to the martyrs and prisoners in Israeli jails.

Only three participants posted blog entries after the initial, obligatory post, and none of these made more than two posts on the blog. The asynchronous mode of communication cannot, therefore, be considered a site of interaction or of identity development and negotiation other than at the outset of the project where it allowed them to position themselves – within the constraints of the programme designers who required them to answer those five questions. These questions index a clear agenda, that is to provide initial output for dialogic discussion on personal, social, and cultural aspects. However, it is in the synchronous dialogue sessions that identities emerge as participants position themselves in relation to others as they engage in interaction.

6.4. The meeting room: synchronous identities

The dialogue group 'met' in Soliya's 'main meeting room' for weekly sessions lasting two hours for seven consecutive weeks[4]. This online meeting room was the situated context for the interactions, where technology mediated the participants' access to one another and even managed to offer a glimpse into one another's local physical surroundings through the small webcam picture (see Figure 6.2 below). This shared space becomes the situated context of interaction, a space in itself with an evolving culture and norms of behaviour of its own which are influenced by a multiplicity of factors: the ideals of its developers who in turn have been influenced by the broader, socio-political context; the technology and its 'affordances' for communication; the individual participants and what they

---

4. This round of the Soliya Connect Program lasted only seven weeks, while it is usually an eight week programme.

bring to the space which is influenced by aspects of what Blommaert (1991) would describe as their 'ethnic habitus'; and aspects of their local contexts on a multiplicity of levels.

6.4.1. Affordances of the meeting room

Figure 6.2. The Soliya videoconferencing interface[5]

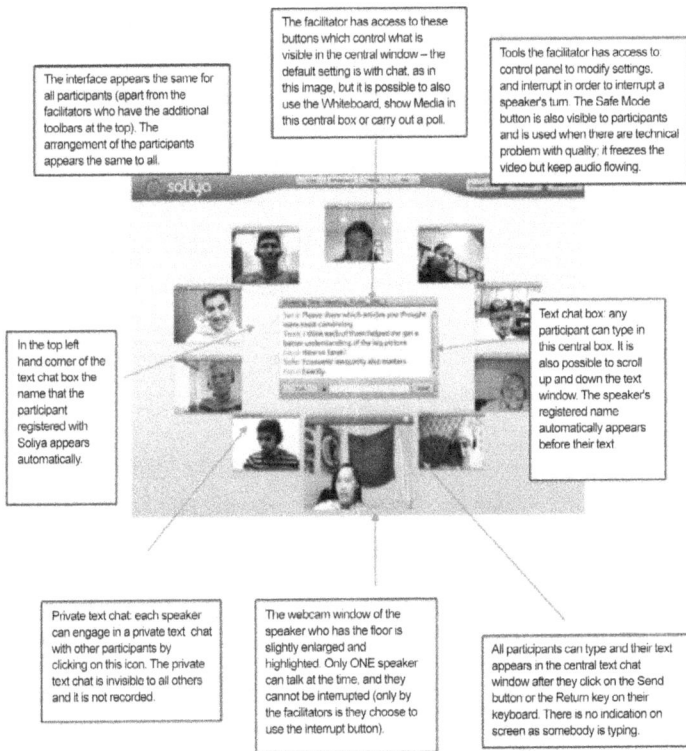

The interface appears the same for all participants (apart from the facilitators who have the additional toolbars at the top). The arrangement of the participants appears the same to all.

The facilitator has access to these buttons which control what is visible in the central window – the default setting is with chat, as in this image, but it is possible to also use the Whiteboard, show Media in this central box or carry out a poll.

Tools the facilitator has access to: control panel to modify settings, and interrupt in order to interrupt a speaker's turn. The Safe Mode button is also visible to participants and is used when there are technical problem with quality: it freezes the video but keep audio flowing.

In the top left hand corner of the text chat box the name that the participant registered with Soliya appears automatically.

Text chat box: any participant can type in this central box. It is also possible to scroll up and down the text window. The speaker's registered name automatically appears before their text

Private text chat: each speaker can engage in a private text chat with other participants by clicking on this icon. The private text chat is invisible to all others and it is not recorded.

The webcam window of the speaker who has the floor is slightly enlarged and highlighted. Only ONE speaker can talk at the time, and they cannot be interrupted (only by the facilitators is they choose to use the interrupt button).

All participants can type and their text appears in the central text chat window after they click on the Send button or the Return key on their keyboard. There is no indication on screen as somebody is typing.

This kind of online situated context has been defined as a glocal space, as the global and local intersect one another in a hybrid and simultaneous manner (Messina

5. Reproduced with kind permissions from © Soliya.

Dahlberg & Bagga-Gupta, 2014). And it is mainly here that the participants' situated identities come into being, through their interactions and also across communication modes, as they make relevant different aspects of their own and others' situated and also transportable identities. This becomes their shared space, where they co-construct their shared history and their emerging group identity develops through the mediation of technology and language.

What is characteristic of the space is first of all its simplicity and minimal distraction from the participants themselves. The way participants are arranged in a circle is intended to create a friendly, non-threatening environment that has affinities to the seating arrangement used for university seminars or 'circle time' in primary schools or therapy groups. In her diary study, Norton (2000/2013) also reports using a circular seating arrangement:

> "We sat in a circle, the configuration of which changed each week [...]. Such a setting, I believe, not only reduced the power differentials between me as a teacher and them as students, but also reframed the women's expectations of whose knowledge was considered more legitimate and valid" (p. 184).

This arrangement is more conducive to dialogue than the hierarchical structure of some virtual learning environments which are specifically designed for teacher-student interaction. In the Soliya platform, at the centre of the circle is the text-chat window to which everybody can contribute. At the bottom of the text chat window is the 'talk' button, which participants need to click on in order to take the floor in audio-video communication. When somebody has the floor, their video window is slightly enlarged, as Sami's is at the bottom centre of the image above. It is not possible for more than one person to speak at a time, so when somebody has the floor they cannot be interrupted through the audio-video mode, though all participants can use the text chat when somebody is speaking. The floor can be requested by clicking on the 'talk' button while somebody is talking, and when participants do this, a small orange button appears on the top right of their window and when the speaker ends their turn, they automatically take the floor.

There is also the possibility for participants to engage in private text chat with one another by clicking on the speech bubble at the top right hand corner of the video window of each participant. This chat is invisible to all other participants and the facilitators too.

The design of the communication, with multiple modes available simultaneously, means that participants need to accomplish their functions both on interactional and also technological levels, and they negotiate the mode of communication as well as meanings and identities. Researchers have found that these different layers of operations can sometimes create 'dislocations' (Liddicoat, 2011); participants can orient towards different modalities and multiple conversations can be carried out at the same time.

Liddicoat (2011) underscores the importance of examining how participants orient to and engage with the technological layer of operations as they construct, understand, and enact their social interaction and, I would add, their multiple identities. How well the participants can manipulate the different interfaces can affect the interaction, as the literature on the 'participation gap' has shown (Jenkins et al., 2009 in Kern, 2014), and which Bali and Bossone (2010) also found in their study on the Soliya context.

The software has been designed in an attempt to address the inevitable imbalances in terms of connectivity when linking participants from across the globe and to create a system which allows for different bandwidths. Yet imbalances do remain, and as Bali and Bossone (2010) report in their study, technical difficulties can limit some students' participation, so they may miss parts of or entire sessions. If they have problems with the microphones or headsets they may have to communicate through text rather than speech, thus perhaps limiting their involvement in discussions. As the researchers report, inevitably the students facing the most technical problems are those from universities with fewer resources, often in the Arab/Muslim region and, they sustain, this empowers the Western-region participants and the well-funded (often Westernised) Arab institutions over the others.

6.4.2. Visual identities

Telles (2009, 2014) has looked at how one's webcam image is a discursive construction – built on the performativity process that draws on the repetition and iteration of codes and symbols, such as gestures, hairstyle, clothes, earrings, make up, and flags (Butler, 1990). All of these will help to produce the emergence of gender, race, national identification, sexual orientation, social class, and most importantly the subject. Clearly the quality and size of the image determines how visible some of these identity markers are, and though webcam technology has been improving, there can be issues such as bandwidth and processing limitations.

Furthermore, in the Soliya platform, the participant windows are quite small as up to 12 or 13 windows may have to be visible at one time and they must all 'fit' on one screen. The more participants there are, the smaller their images and also the chance that part of the window will be overlapping with other windows. The size of the computer screen one is using also determines the size of the image[6]. In most cases, there is only the head and shoulders of the participants visible of the screen and a very limited amount of the background context.

Despite its limitations, the webcam image does, nonetheless, offer visual cues as regards elements of interactants' 'transportable identities'. The screenshot below (Figure 6.3) comes from the recording of the first session (faces have been pixelated to anonymise the participants). Visible identity markers present indicate religion, gender (as in the case of the hijab, indexing Muslim and female identity, long hair female identity), and can also index political allegiances/beliefs – for example solidarity with Palestinian resistance as in the case of the keffiyeh which one of the participants is wearing (though it could be interpreted as a fashion item).

---

6. There are several other factors which can influence the quality of the images we see on the interface, and these include bandwidth, quality of the webcam, lighting (the amount of light and whether it is front or back lighting) and the position of the camera.

The 'transportable identities' which are indexed by these markers are available to participants (and the analyst) but this does not mean that they are necessarily made relevant by the interactants during the interactions. Indeed in this study, which adopted an emic approach, they were only considered in the interactional analysis **when** they were oriented to by the participants.

Figure 6.3. Positioning in relation to webcams[7]

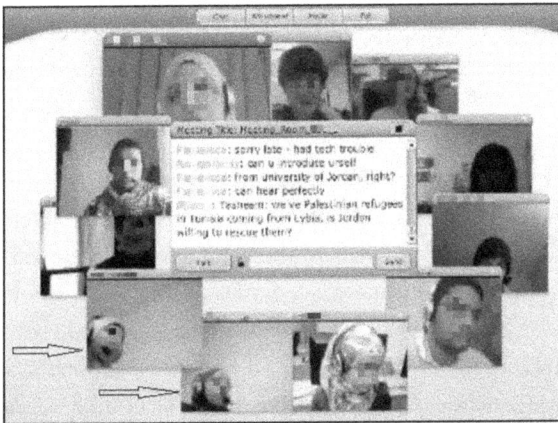

6.4.3. Gaze and positioning

As Kern (2015) points out, "real eye contact does not exist online" (p. 345) for if one wants to create the illusion of looking into one's interlocutor's eyes in videoconferencing they have to look directly at the webcam rather than their interlocutor. However, the use of a webcam can and often does create a sense of proximity and even intimacy (Telles, 2009). Kern (2015) points out that the closer a speaker is to the webcam the more involved they appear to be, and indeed in exploring the data I found that often when a participant is speaking they will move closer to the camera. Clarity of the image is an important issue.

7. Reproduced with kind permissions from © Soliya.

Some participants can be seen very clearly with facial expressions that can easily be interpreted, whilst others have a very pixelated image.

In Figure 6.3 above, all of the participants present are relatively close to their webcams, with Jessica furthest away. As regards gaze, we can see that some participants appear to be looking directly at their interactants as their webcams seem to be positioned slightly above the level of their eyes (possibly incorporated on top of the screens of the computers they are using). Others seem to be looking in a different direction, that is their gazes are not directed towards their webcams, though we assume they are looking at their computer screens.

The framing of the participants, that is their position in relation to their webcams can be determined by the participants to a greater or lesser extent. It is partly established by technical issues such as whether the webcam is fixed or moveable, but even with fixed webcams there is a degree of flexibility, and users can, and often do, exercise a degree of agency in how they position themselves in relation to the webcam (Sindoni, 2013). The inset window with one's own face, the 'contre-champ' (Guichon & Cohen, 2016), offers a form of 'visual mirroring', as Malinowski and Kramsch (2014) define it, an "ever-present reflection of the self" (p. 20). This can have a distracting effect, as these authors found, or it can be seen to support identity construction, and the framing and positioning of oneself in the interactions (Telles, 2009)[8].

The importance of framing for some of the participants in this situated context emerges as some of the participants purposefully placed the camera so that their

---

8. In his study of the contribution of webcam images to teletandem sessions (which entail one to one student interaction through video-conferencing and a somewhat different situated context as there are only two interlocutors, hence attention is more focussed on the image which is also larger), Telles (2009) found that the majority of the 22 students that participated in his survey study reported that they took care to control the framing of their own image, how much of the background (their physical and 'cultural' space) was made visible and making technical adjustments to correct it if necessary. Telles (2009) also reports that most students found webcams to give them greater security and self-confidence in conversation though some students had unfavourable opinions about the use of webcam images as they found them intrusive "by exposing feelings, gestures and reactions that they preferred to hide from their partners" (p. 71). Research which has been carried out as regards the use of the webcam in pedagogical contexts has found framing to constitute a 'crucial element'; what the online teacher chooses to show can personalise the relationship with the learner and has been found to facilitate comprehension and involvement (Guichon & Cohen, 2016). It can be assumed that the webcam has some impact on the interaction in the Soliya configuration, though the higher number of participants and therefore images and also reduced size may mitigate the effect.

heads appear only in the lower left hand corner of their window and at an angle. They appear to be deliberately removing themselves from the centre stage of their window, avoiding others' gazes and the level of proximity and intimacy that the webconferencing can entail (Kern, 2014; Telles, 2009). It is interesting that these two participants also failed to publish a photo of themselves in the Soliya blogs, thus reflecting an alignment between their identities in these modes and a dispreference for the visual mode.

The webcam allows a small part of the participants' local spaces to enter the shared online space as the background is partly visible in the small windows. In most cases there is little to see, but the local context is always somehow a part of the communication and can be oriented to by the participants in many ways.

In the first session, the facilitators set up an activity called 'where in the world' which invites participants to move their webcams around the room they are in to show the other participants where they are connecting from and they share a part of their local (transportable) identities. Jessica models this activity for the others in Turn 13 in the excerpt below (Table 6.2).

Table 6.2. Session 1, Turn 13

Turn	Speaker	Audio	Text chat
13	Jessica	'hh ok so emm while ( ) for the others (2s) to connect (...) >to hook in with us< there should be umm (2s) 'hh three or four other people, em shall we just try doing a round and we can ea:ch introduce ourselves? and so (...) a little bit (2s) emm and and show a little bit of about our environment about our environment. I'm in my office as you can see, can you see ? oops hehh and outside it's raining (...) it's a really horrible day ok (..) Can you show us >a little bit about where you are?<	

As she speaks she moves the webcam around the room she is in and out of the window, commenting on the rain outside and showing that she is in her office, but she does not say what kind of office it is, in what town or country, or what job she does. Without formulating an explicit description of her identity or her geopolitical location she has, however, disclosed a small amount of information about her transportable identity, that she is not a student, but rather somebody who works in an office, but it is not clear what kind of office this is, nor her role in this office.

By moving the webcams around the rooms they are connecting from and sharing information about their immediate environments, through the 'hors-champ' the participants make relevant different aspects of their identities. As the participants follow Jessica's example, many of them implicitly orient to their identities as students, for Kate's room is messy as she is preparing for a 'school trip' to Dubai, Deni is in a 'dorm room', and Fadela in a library, whilst Jack shows his family home as it is 'spring break'. Through the mediation of the webcam, participants have a glimpse into each other's immediate contexts, their local worlds.

The activity 'where in the world' highlights the boundaries between the different local, physical spaces which come together in a shared, virtual space, the situated context of Soliya. Through this activity, participants oriented to each others' physical spaces and showed alignment and adequation to the transportable identities of students that they all had in common. Following Jessica's example, participants oriented to the visual mode and their immediate physical environment which could be framed by their webcams. The local spaces participants caught a glimpse of through this activity are present throughout the interactions in the three sessions analysed, however blurred or distant they may be, through the background noises that can be heard as participants speak, and also by the way they may determine what participants say and even how they say it. Speaking from a shared dorm room with a roommate present, or from a computer in an Internet cafe in a country which is experiencing political upheaval is not the same as speaking from a private space, though of course the impact it had on the interactions cannot be determined.

The fact that Jack was connecting at 5 o'clock in the morning was made relevant several times in the interactions and through the visual mode. He would often rub his eyes and hair and "do being sleepy" which came to characterise Jack's identity as "funny/sleepy Jack". At the same time it could be seen to authenticate

Jack's identity as a committed member of the group by highlighting his dedication to the project by getting up so early to participate (see the Table 6.3 below).

Table 6.3. Session 3, Turns 29-33

Turn	Speaker	Audio	Text chat
29	Jessica	so what time is it in in for you Jack? five in the morning?	
30	silence	(5s)	
31	Jack	yeah five in the morning it's been exciting (.) I've been talking to my friends about these sesssions and they're like 'hh oh my gosh that's way too early I would ne:ver do that 'hh so yeah that's um interesting	
32	silence	(3s)	
33	Jessica	hh we:ll we appreciate your dedication and commitment yeah I don't think I could do it at five o'clock in the morning eh ha ha I wouldn't function he he	

Temporal and physical locations (TimeSpace) also become, as Messina Dahlberg and Bagga-Gupta (2015) point out, important referents through which students frame their positioning inside the online space but also at the boundary of different online and offline communities. The TimeSpace dimension of this space is what the participants have in common and comes to embody their shared history and their collective identity. Through the webcam this is enacted in part through the visual language they collectively acquire – for instance the 'thumbs up' gesture to index they can hear one another, the air quotes gesture when they are aware they are using a contentious term, and waving goodbye as they take leave of the space.

6.4.4. Oral identities

The voice is an important channel of non-verbal communication because it delivers paralinguistic cues such as tone of voice, intonation, pitch, and speech rate. These are important elements to which a great deal of attention is paid in some forms of social linguistic analysis such as conversation analysis. There are conventions for representing qualities such as speed of delivery, hesitations, and false starts in transcripts – and I have adopted some of these in the transcription process at various points, so there are aspects of the speakers' identities that emerge, though their impact on the reader is limited compared to the effect of hearing the audio on the listener.

Jack, for example, emerges as an insecure speaker whose speech is characterised by disfluencies such as hesitation and false starts. The extract below (Table 6.4), which comes after he has been asked by Thamena why he wrote that Israel was fortunate in response to a word associations activity, is just one of many examples of Jack's speaker identity. He was an active speaker and took the floor many times, his turns were long but characterised by redundancy. However, he showed a preference for the audio mode to the text chat, as there were a few occasions when he was called upon to speak through text, and could have oriented to this mode, but preferred the audio.

Table 6.4. Session 3, Turn 240

Turn	Speaker	Audio	Text chat
240	Jack	ok erm I fortunate because: I'm not exactly sure why: erm everybody's hehh well everybody I mean (.) like the West has decided to support (1s) Israel so much and I mean cos I can see (.) that the relationships between Israel and Palestine and other places is not a good one so I'm not exactly sure why (2s) we've been supporting them so I said fortunate because (s) (.) it means kind of lucky for them I guess like (4s) yeah but Israel's lucky and I don't necessa I don't think it's fair I think yeah we need to do something to (4s) well er but the West should be more aware and it er willing to hel- to make a difference? I gue- make a positive difference like settle the (4s) not the er controversy er not controversy erm sol(ve) the dispute? I guess I mean cos I want it to stop yeah	Jessica: Jack - not exactly sure why Jessica: 'the "West" has decided to support Israel so much Jessica: I can see the relatiohsip with Palestine is not a good one Jessica: so in terms of that relationship Jessica: Israel is lucky - the more powerful

Though Jack is a 'native speaker' of English, his turns are not always clear and coherent as he appears insecure of the terminology to use, he searches for words and makes a lot of false starts and repairs. This may be due to his lack of familiarity with content and fear of upsetting or offending his interlocutors (as he reported in the final session).

Whilst hesitation and false starts can be included in transcriptions without too much difficulty, accent is difficult, if not impossible at times, to convey through transcription, hence that Brendan speaks with a North Carolina accent, or that Jessica speaks with a British accent and Thamena with a Jordanian one does not emerge from the transcript. One might ask whether accent is important for identity construction in the online space, and I would argue that it is, for accent can index aspects related to transportable identities relating to people's origins or life trajectories (in terms of region, social class…) and *may* influence how participants orient to one another.

However, as I have said previously, aspects of identity become relevant in this study only if and when interactants orient to them explicitly or implicitly. For example, if a participant asks to be corrected or asks another how something should be pronounced, they are orienting to the other's expert speaker identity (Liddicoat & Tudini, 2013) and making relevant their non-expert identity.

6.4.5. Constraints

For the participants, interacting through the audio mode was not straightforward since it is quite unlike face to face communication where one simply speaks. They had to click on the 'Talk' button and remember to click on it again once they had finished talking. Furthermore, in order to take the floor, that is to be heard, they had to wait for the floor to be free as it is not technically possible for participants to interrupt.

Furthermore, there were often issues linked to the *quality* of the audio, which can hinder understanding. The quality of audio is determined to a large degree by the quality of the Internet infrastructure (bandwidth capacity) which, in turn, is influenced by geopolitical factors. North America and Europe are high bandwidth regions and have the top shares of global bandwidth. The Middle East's bandwidth is very low in comparison, though it is growing[9]. Palestinian telecommunications are under the control of Israel as it is Israel that allocates frequencies, determines where infrastructure can be built and allocates bandwidth for internet use[10]. Capping bandwidth, slowing down traffic and even suspending Internet access are measures which (as well as limited infrastructure) affect the Internet's functionality and thus can limit free expression – and this is something which repressive governments often do. If we consider in particular the power attributed to social networks in the so-called Arab Spring it would not be surprising to learn that such measures were taken in Egypt and Tunisia. Whether or not this was indeed the cause, the quality of audio for Fadela (in Palestine), Rana, and Mohammed (in Egypt) was particularly poor with fuzziness and interference making them at times incomprehensible, and they regularly disappeared from the meeting room due to connectivity problems. Alef's audio was not of bad quality though he was connecting from Tunisia, and Kate who was connecting from Qatar had a generally good connection. The quality of the audio of the students connecting from the US was generally excellent, there was no background noise or interference. Jessica was connecting from Italy, and the quality of the audio was generally acceptable. The negative impact technological issues can have on students' participation and engagement in the Soliya Connect Program has been reported by Bali (2013, 2014).

6.4.6. Written/text identities

I now explore how participants and facilitators oriented to the text chat in their identity construction. By coding and quantifying the main discourse functions for which facilitators and participants used the text chat I conceptualised the discourse identities created through this mode, which also served to acquire a better understanding of the situated identities of facilitators and participants.

---

9. https://www.telegraph.co.uk/travel/maps-and-graphics/countries-with-fastest-internet-connection-speeds/

10. https://www.tikkun.org/nextgen/beyond-walls-and-checkpoints-the-digital-occupation-of-palestine

Throughout the sessions we see the facilitators orienting to the identity of transcribers as one of them transcribes a summary of what is being said while the other leads the dialogue. In the example below (Table 6.5), we see transcription 'in action', as Jessica types what Ranà is saying. In the second line of text, in Turn 161 where she is transcribing, she indexes orientation to this identity by writing Ranà's name followed by a dash, and then we can see in the following lines she is still transcribing, though she doesn't write Ranà's name on every line. She closes her transcription of Ranà in Turn 162 with a 'smiling face' emoticon, a way of showing her alignment with Ranà's words using the affordances of the text chat.

Table 6.5. Session 1, Turns 161-164

Turn	Speaker	Spoken	Text chat
161	Ranà	(2s) well guys I just want to tell you that we have another person who is supposed to be communicating with us but they are taking some technical problems ( ) in their internet lab and they will try and be there shortly? I just want to tell you some more about our role (...) as facilitators, me and Jessica? we are here just to support you to give you the quick directions you are totally free to speak about er whatever topic you want? you are totally free to express your opinion ? we are here just to support and organising	10:22 Jessica: Great Mohammed 10:40 Jessica: Ranà - a little more about our role 10:45 Jessica: We are here to support you 10:48 Jessica: give the group directons
162	silence	(34s)	10:56 Jessica: you're totally free to express your opinoins 10:59 Jessica: ask what you want 11:12 Jessica: we're here to help you along 11:15 Jessica: and organize sometimes :-)
163	Jessica	OK and Kate?	

| 164 | Kate | (3s) yup, so I heard about Soliya from my professor, I'm taking (so sociology) (.) this year 'hh and erm I think cos we have a choice (..) either do research or do Soliya so I chose Soliya since I heard from erm the er my colleagus that Soliya is a great opportunity to know more about people even though I live in a very diverse country I (5s) ya - even though I live in a very diverse country? I still want to think (..) I still want to KNOW what other people think (.) in other countries. | 11:34 Alef: suggestion: the issue of the refugees on the Tunisian-Lybian borders? 12:02 Jessica: Kate - have choice, research of soliya 12:09 Jessica: is studying theology – right? 12:16 Kate: sociology 12:21 Jessica: Heard from colleagues that Soliya is great opportunity 12:24 Jessica: ok sorry, sociology |

There are several ways in which the facilitator-transcriber indexes that she is transcribing others' words. The most common way is described above, with the name of the speaker followed by a colon and then the transcription following through a series of lines without the name being repeated every time.

The transcriber is in a sense acting as 'interpreter' of the events for others, as what she writes is necessarily selective. It is important that the transcriber understands what is being said in order to provide a written record of interaction, hence checking comprehension and requesting repetition are activities which display an orientation to the identity of transcriber and facilitator of understanding for the others. In the extract above, for example, we see in Turn 164 Jessica uses the text chat to check her understanding ("is studying theology – right?"), and Kate corrects her ("sociology").

Understanding is an interactional achievement and is closely related to issues of face (Hamilton, 1994; Heritage, 1988, in Antaki & Widdicombe, 1998, p. 177). Failure to understand and repeatedly requesting repetition can be face-threatening and could suggest that the interactants' English language competence is not adequate, thus making relevant their 'learner' or 'non-native speaker' status. In many international or lingua franca settings there is often an orientation *not* to topicalise others' language production and instead to engage in practices such as 'let it pass' and 'make it normal' (Firth, 1996), which are used to deflect attention from linguistic hurdles. These strategies are occasionally used by the facilitators when their task of facilitating understanding through transcription is not jeopardised. However, there are many occasions when the facilitators are transcribing and need to check understanding of what is being said. Often they apologise and account for their lack of comprehension, attributing it to poor quality audio, as in the example below. This accounting for their request serves to protect both their face and that of their interlocutors.

> Jessica: Doja - focussed on her opinion
> Jessica: the revolution, and the hope of the people
> Jessica: is that right? Sound not great

Sometimes the facilitators also account for their comprehension checks or difficulties in transcription by assigning it to the speed of delivery, thus indexing participants' failure to adequate their speech to the international context, a characteristic that has been ascribed to the 'monolingual native speaker' (Jenkins, 2014). This use of the text chat allows the facilitators to highlight the need for the speaker to adapt their speech to the context, in a non-threatening way.

> Jessica: middle name is Adam
> Jessica: relating to man, right?
> Jessica: You were speaking too fast for me to type!
> Jack: Yes

There are several instances in the text chat transcripts where some of the participants explicitly index the facilitator-transcriber identity and the use of chat in supporting their understanding. For example, they may specifically ask for transcription, as in the example below.

> Mohammed: sorry can u write it down
> Ranà: well no worries mouhammad
> Mohammed: ok thanks
> Fadela: write plz

6.5. Group identity

Through the qualitative analysis of the text chat it was possible to see how as the participants get to know one another better and as the sessions progress, more of them use this medium of text to engage in phatic communication. We can see this from the salutations at the end of the first session when Alef, who is the first to take his leave, sets an example, with a friendly, informal tone and emoticon. Others respond to Alef, many aligning to the same friendly tone, and adequating to his expressive use of chat with emoticons and abbreviations, in particular Thamena and Fadela.

> Alef: I gotta go :) see u guys
> Jessica: great - although it ws the first meetin
> Jessica: it wasn't that difficult
> Thamena: nice to meet u all :)
> Thamena: bye Alaf :)
> Jack: By e Alaf!
> Alef: salutations from Tunisia with love ;)
> Mohammed: bye Alaf
> Maawaa: bye gues thank you all
> Denise: I also have to go! bye, thank you!
> Thamena: ok see you all then
> Thamena: tc
> Thamena: :)
> Jessica: nice to meet you all
> Thamena: bye
> Jessica: and am really looking forward to seeing you again next week
> Mohammed: thanx every one again and bye
> Fadela: c u alll byeeeee
> Jack: I will see you all next week! byenext

This phatic use of the text chat, for greetings and leave-taking, offering encouragement to one another and expressing feelings through emoticons indexes the emergence of a group identity. As the sessions progress this seems to be increasingly marked and gradually involves more and more of the participants who align to this use of text and participants' use of text chat as the following extract from the beginning of Session 7 shows.

Kate: hello miss Jessica
Mohammed: hi
Jessica: Hi Mohammed
Kate: hi
Ranà: hey there
Mohammed: hi Ranà
Kate: hi
Ranà: Jack
Ranà: good morning
Kate: nice hair cut :)
Ranà: yeah
Mohammed: hi Jack
Jessica: Hi Fadela
Jack: hey Mohammed :)
Fadela: hiiiiiiiiiiii
Kate: hi
Fadela: nice Jack :P
Mohammed: hi
Jack: hey
Jessica: Kate - you have the mike - why don't you ask a question
Ranà: hi maawa
Fadela: mmmmmm
Fadela: forgot :|
Fadela: preparing for the finals!!
Kate: when is it?
Jessica: Hi Thamena abd Maawa
Ranà: hi Thamena
Ranà: hey Dojaq
Doja: hi everybody
Kate: good luck!

> Thamena: hii all :)
> Fadela: thx :)
> Jessica: try your mikes Thamena and Doja and Maawa
> Fadela: hiii thmeeeeeeeenaa
> Thamena: hiiiiiiii fadeee
> Thamena: u r talking about finals :S

We see Fadela and Thamena using repeated letters, abbreviations (thx) and emoticons as they interact with others, and in particular with one another, perhaps affirming their identity as friends through this playful language (Kern, 2015, p. 109).

In the opening of the session even Kate and Jack, who until now had rarely used these phatic forms of text communication, use smileys, indexing group alignment through these discursive resources.

Other forms of phatic communication, largely through the text chat and which index the emergence of group identity are thanking, particularly used by the facilitators as follow-ups to responses and also the word 'great' or expressions like "that's great" (in bold below) which index a friendly supportive group identity.

> Jessica: sees it as a great opportunity
> Jessica: what are you hoping to gain from it
> Jessica: Jack - see other people's viewpoints
> Jessica: Jack: more personal insight
> **Jessica: that's great! Thanks**
> Jessica: What do you expect to gain from Soliya?
> Jessica: Alef_ same as Jack
> Jessica: heard from classmate
> Jessica: excited about this opportunity to talk about issues that all humans share
> Jessica: like religion, politics,
> Jessica: exciting to meet others from other parts of the world

Jessica: and what they think of me, my country and people
Jessica: Thanks Alef

In the analysis above I have identified affective indicators such as emotion and humour, interactive features such as greetings and salutations, vocatives, and cohesive indicators such as acknowledgement, approval, and invitation to participate (orchestration). All of these uses of text chat are markers of social presence or community indicators and can be seen to index participants' orientation to an online group identity (Kehrwald, 2010, p. 47).

Facilitator identities

In this chapter, I explore the situated and discourse identities of *facilitators*, how they discursively construct this identity and how they position themselves and others in the interactions. More importantly I seek to illustrate through examples the impact this has on the interactions and the participants' orientations to identities as they evolve through the programme.

We rarely use category labels to identify ourselves, rather it is through our actions and discourses in specific settings that we perform identities. Doctors take on their professional identity as they ask questions regarding their patients' health, teachers do this by giving instructions, initiating and directing interactions with students, and offering feedback (Gardner, 2012; Hall & Walsh, 2002; Heritage, 2012; Richards, 2006). The facilitators in this situated context perform a series of actions and discourse identities in the Soliya meeting room.

In this chapter, I provide brief extracts from the online interactions which serve to illustrate how the two co-facilitators, Ranà and Jessica, discursively establish their situated identities. They do this by orienting to the identities of:

- *hosts*, welcoming participants and making them feel at home in this online space, troubleshooting as they dealt with any technical issues hindering the conversation and transcribing summaries of what was said, and also seeing participants out of the space;

- *implementers* of an institutional agenda as they have participants engage in specific activities (from the Soliya Connect Program Online Curriculum) and initiate and guide conversations about a range of issues;

- *orchestrators of interaction*, supporting the turn taking mechanics of the discussions and ensuring that all participants are given the opportunity to speak;

- *summarisers and probers*, offering summaries of what the different participants were saying, and probing as they followed up responses with further questions or challenges, enhancing the quality of the interactions by getting the discussion to dig deeper and facilitating mutual learning;

- *reflexive practitioners,* reflecting with the participants on the group process.

7.1. Facilitators as 'hosts' and 'experts' in the online space

Online spaces, particularly those in which synchronous communication tools are used, can be likened to physical spaces in that one has to 'enter' and 'leave' the space, and also interact with others within this space. In fact, metaphors of space and place are commonly used in talking about online communities (for example White & Le Cornu, 2011).

The Soliya 'meeting room', as the name suggests, is a small, intimate online space. Participants need to acquire an understanding of the conventions of this community and the technologies used for communication. They need to become pragmatically and 'semiotically agile' (Thorne, Sauro, & Smith, 2015) in order to be able to perform identities within this context, and the facilitators play an important role in supporting them in this.

The facilitators are more 'at home' than participants in this space as they already have a degree of familiarity with the workings of it and they take on the identity of 'hosts' and 'experts'. They are present in the space at the beginning of every session and greet the participants as they arrive, and also see the participants out of the space as the session ends.

The facilitators in this study, Jessica and Ranà, use all communication modes available to them to greet participants. At the beginning of the sessions they use both the spoken and the written channels to welcome participants, encouraging them to also speak so that any technical issues can be addressed. If participants arrive once discussions are underway the facilitators often choose to use the text mode to acknowledge the appearance of participants so that they do not interrupt the flow of discussion, and then take advantage of natural pauses in the interaction to greet through the spoken mode.

The virtual space is indeed referred to as if it were a physical space, with facilitators using temporal and spatial indexical markers, such as 'this', 'here', and also verbs such as 'meet' and 'gone'. In the extract below (Table 7.1), for example, Jessica tells the participants "it's great to meet you" (Turn 63) as if they were together in the same place. She acknowledges technical difficulties the group are having, but she then orients to a more expert role and indicates the ways in which they can use the affordances of the environment to communicate, for example using thumbs up to indicate when they can hear and text chat when they are having trouble. She also encourages the participants to ask each other questions – and to take ownership of the space; "this is your space (..) and we're here to help you along", explicitly alluding to the facilitators' institutional role in this space.

Table 7.1. Session 1, Turn 63

Turn	Speaker	Audio	Text chat
63	Jessica	'hh great (..) well it's great to meet you all.. we can kind of < see each other >, it takes a bit of getting used to with the technology, 'hh erm (.) we can see each other but >I don't know about you< my pictures are sometimes very pixelated (.) so the image isn't always very clear 'hh (..) but the camera's very useful (.) so erm: you know thumbs up when you can hear? ok? erm if there are any problems 'hh you can use the text box? and () please feel free to ask each others and ask anybody any questions because this is your space (..) we're here to 'hh help you along (..) ok? 'hh let's start 'hh let's try again to see my Rana my cofacilitator if you can hear her?	

She uses a language which is specific to this context (the directive 'thumbs up' may appear somewhat unusual in most face to face situations). The 'thumbs up' or 'thumbs down' gesture indeed becomes part of the visual language of the group in this space and recurs throughout the sessions when participants are asked to provide a yes/no response to a question – often a technical question. This gesture appears to be almost a standard form of visual communication in video-conferencing as other researchers have reported (Guichon & Wigham, 2016).

The facilitator as host is responsible for making participants feel at home, doing what they can to ensure the participants' understanding and ability to contribute to the discussions. This discourse identity of host emerges also through the phatic use of the text chat for greetings and leave-taking, offering encouragement and managing the turns in this online space.

7.2. Implementers of institutional agendas: indexing and authorisation of situated identities

Ranà and Jessica do not explicitly identify themselves as facilitators until Turn 69, about 20 minutes after the start of the first session, when Jessica explains that there should be two facilitators working together (Table 7.2). However, it was clear from the beginning that they were indeed the facilitators through their discourse identities. In the extract below, we see how Jessica indexes her situated identity (Turn 67) by making relevant 'the goals of the programme' and explaining how they will go about achieving these goals through the dialogue. Here she highlights first of all the institutional aspect of her situated identity as she delivers what we could call the 'Soliya agenda' (Boden & Zimmerman, 1991).

There are many hesitations in this extended turn, lasting up to five seconds, and Jessica repeatedly checks understanding by saying ok with a rising intonation. Her unnaturalness suggests she is not quite comfortable in what she is saying, as if she is using an institutional script which she has not quite mastered. This is confirmed by looking at the visual mode as at times she seems to be reading, her gaze is directed downwards and 'hors champ', that is outside of the frame (Guichon & Wigham, 2016), and at times we can actually see that she is holding a piece of paper.

Table 7.2. Session 1, Turns 67-69

Turn	Speaker	Audio	Text chat
67	Jessica	'hh ok In that case I'll just spend one or two minutes explaining to you (..) the goals of the programme (.) ok? erm are you all following me, can you hear? (2s) Ya? ok hh erm If you want me to slow down (.) type in something in the text box ok (.) so you can give me an indication (.) if you're following me or not (...) (5s) erm so basically the go:als of the Soliya Connect Program as you know? (1s) are to erm (..) increase understanding and awareness? ok? e: m for the perspectives? and narratives? of other people in the group 'hh erm also part of the process ((clear throat)) (you gain) it will help us to gain more of an understanding of our own (..) perspectives and where they come from 'hh where we're coming from too ok? hh erm (1s) and hopefully through (.) the di:alogue process we will build relationships ok with one another we'll get to know each other a bit better hh (1s) erm ((clear throat)) as you know there's also the video project 'hh which we'll talk about (.) at the end of the project at the end of the session toda:y (..) ok? hh for the video project you'll (4s) be have you'll be creating your own video ( ) media literacy skills (3s) ok? (..) erm (..) and then finally? the idea is that we create a sense of empowerment and erm so that we can develop a long term in interest in the relationship (.) between? western world ok? and the predominantly Arab and Muslim world ok (..) and we'll talk later on today about the various labels which we use (2) 'hh is that clear?	Brendan: yes
68	silence	(11s)	
69	Jessica	'hh now there should be two facilitators ok, and we we alternate in helping each other 'hh erm so ((cough)) but Ranà is having some technical problems hh, when I type when I speak she would be typing (2s) ok so there should be a written record of what's going on 'hh (..) but there seem to be some technical problems (..) 'hh if you want me to type ok just write in the text box, ask me to type	

Many of the words and expressions Jessica uses echo those that appear in the Soliya website and programme objectives as discussed in Chapter 5: *increased understanding and awareness, perspectives, narratives, our own perspectives, build relationships, media literacy skills, western, predominantly Arab and Muslim, empowerment*. Jessica is appropriating the language of Soliya, what we could call 'Soliya-speak', as she performs the institutional identity of the facilitator, though as said above, her performance is somewhat hesitant and unnatural at times, perhaps not having yet taken ownership of this institutional language. Her hesitations also suggest lack of confidence with the terminology used to frame the discussion. Her closing words in this turn make reference to the issue of terminology as she tells the group they will talk about the 'labels' used later during the session, alluding to the Soliya agenda.

Jessica's use of pronouns in addressing the group varies, as she switches between **you** and **we** (highlighted also in the extract). When she checks understanding and talks about the activities participants will have to do independently she uses the second person to address the participants, but when she talks about the dialogue process she tends to use the first person plural pronoun **we**. This use of the first person plural pronoun indexes shared goals and it projects the intended outcomes of the programme onto the whole group as they are all called upon to invest in this joint activity. The participants are indexed as agents who will jointly carry out the actions Jessica proposes. In this turn she also hints at the 'imagined identities' that the Soliya Connect Program prefigures for participants, that is young people with a long term interest in the relationship between 'Western societies' and 'predominantly Arab and Muslim societies'.

Later on in this same session R$\`a$na also makes explicit reference to the situated identity of the facilitators (Turn 161, Table 7.3), indexing the facilitator-host by the use of the spatial marker 'here', saying that her and Jessica are 'here' in order to support the participants and offer directions and some organisation, but that the participants are free to talk about what they want and are free to express their opinions. In the excerpt below we see the facilitators Ranà and Jessica working in tandem, for as Ranà speaks, Jessica types a summary of what she is saying. Ranà seems to be explaining the 'rules of engagement' (Goffman, 1963, in Blommaert, 2015, p. 2), orienting to expert identity as she clarifies the specific roles of the actors and the situated identities of the facilitators and participants in this online space. Jessica, on the other hand, orients to the transcriber, which is part of the institutional identity of facilitators mentioned in the previous chapter.

Table 7.3. Session 1, Turns 161-162

Turn	Speaker	Audio	Text chat
161	Ranà	(2s) well guys I just want to tell you that we have another person who is supposed to be communicating with us but they are taking some technical problems ( ) in their internet lab and they will try and be there shortly? I just want to tell you some more about our role (...) as facilitators, me and Jessica? we are here just to support you to give you the quick directions you are totally free to speak about er whatever topic you want? you are totally free to express your opinion? we are here just to support and organising	Jessica: Great Mohammed Jessica: Ranà - a little more about our role Jessica: We are here to support you Jessica: give the group directons
162	silence	(20s)	Jessica: you're totally free to express your opinoins Jessica: ask what you want Jessica: we're here to help you along Jessica: and organize sometimes :-)

There are a total of 18 instances in the three sessions analysed when the facilitators explicitly index their institutional identity by making reference to the curriculum, planned activities for the sessions, their responsibilities, reading tasks, and assignments. In explicitly using the label 'facilitator', referring to the institutional programme and using the language that is associated with Soliya, Ranà and Jessica can be seen as engaging in the *authorisation* of these identities and of the actions they take. This authorisation is necessary as the discourse identities of discussion initiator, asker of questions, and orchestrator of interaction, which I will explore in the next section, can be potentially face-threatening (Brown & Levinson, 1987) if one does not have the authority to perform them and they could thus be dismissed or ignored by the participants. The facilitators are not teachers in a familiar classroom context, they are online dialogue facilitators, a figure that participants are unlikely to have come across in other contexts, hence the need to define their role and 'authorise' the actions they take by making reference to institutional identities.

Another important characteristic of the facilitator identity in this study is that there are two of them and they share the responsibilities, as explicitly mentioned by both Jessica and Ranà in the interactions reported above. They work in tandem – for example with one facilitator leading the discussion while the other transcribes to support the learners. Like all facilitators, for every session they plan an outline of their session and organise their co-facilitation so that ideally whilst one leads an activity the other transcribes, thus providing support for participants' understanding.

The Soliya sessions in fact are not 'naturally occurring conversations', but rather semi-structured interactions which the co-facilitators have planned in advance with the support of the 'Online Curriculum' (Soliya, 2010). As the Soliya Connect Program is integrated into some university curricula and student participants may gain official recognition, there is a need for clear goals and some consistency in students' experiences across the multiple dialogue groups. The online curriculum provides an array of tools which include discussion questions and suggestions on a range of topics that the facilitators can choose from. The suggested activities and teaching tools are designed to take groups through the online dialogue process that is the basis of Soliya's Connect Program. In certain weeks of the exchange there are some recommended activities that all dialogue groups[1] engage in, other weeks the groups themselves are left to establish the topics to be discussed with the facilitators.

Each session generally follows a similar structure in that there are ice-breaking activities at the beginning of a session, some activities or questions on specific topics, and a final closing round with reflections on the session. The aim is for the

---

1. At the time of the study there were around 30 discussion groups. At the time of writing this book there are over 100 groups per semester.

groups to gradually take ownership of the dialogue and collaboratively engage in knowledge construction by sharing their personal experiences, and becoming curious to learn more about the contexts and situations they hear about.

7.3. Facilitator/orchestrator of interaction

The mediating role of technology imposes some constraints on the communication, as discussed in Chapter 6, for example allowing only one person to speak at a time, but at the same time making multiple floors available at once (e.g. spoken and written modes), which can lead to parallel conversations. The framed image through the webcam does not have many of the visual contextual cues which are present in face to face contexts, such as gaze and bodily movements which can signal or prepare conversational moves (Androutsopoulos, 2013).

Throughout the first half of the first session, and indeed at different moments of all the sessions, the facilitators orient to the 'orchestrator's of interaction' identity using a range of different strategies to facilitate the turn-taking. Sometimes this is a response to participants specifically asking for directions, which can result from extended silences as in the example below from early on in the first session.

Jessica initiates the interaction with an activity in which participants are asked about the meaning of their names (Turn 78, Table 7.4). After a 24 second silence, Brendan asks if there is any order to follow as regards responses (Turn 80) and Jessica says no, whoever wants to speak can. Brendan then responds to the question that Jessica had asked, after which there is silence lasting nine seconds before Jessica elicits another speaker by saying 'next?' in an interrogative tone (Turn 88). This too is followed by a long silence (15 seconds) which is interrupted by Brendan who in a low tone of voice says "are you all there y'all there" (Turn 90). Jessica then once again orients to the discourse identity of 'orchestrator of interaction' (Turn 92) by saying they will "do a round" and nominates the first speaker of this round, Mohammed. This way of organising turns in rounds, which is repeated several times during the sessions, indexes the 'space' of interaction, the circular configuration of the participants in this online space. It is also one of the suggested strategies in the training manual for facilitators and is used to ensure participation of all students.

Table 7.4. Session 1, Turns 78-92

Turn	Speaker	Audio	Text chat
78	Jessica	(5s) ok so Ranà we've just done a little round of where in the world we are? erm: (2s) and now >whashall we do< erm talk about what our names mean (..) what people's names means? if your names have a meaning? Ranà (our) where are you?	
79	silence	(24s)	Ranà: sorry guys if you can't hear me
80	Brendan	are we going in any order? or anything	
81	silence	(10s)	Jessica: we could hear Ranà Ranà: you but some tech issues
82	Jessica	erm: no whoever wants to speak (.) so ok Simon he he as you volunteered does your name have a meaning?	Ranà: Wow Ranà: great news
83	silence	(3s)	
84	Brendan	No actually my name is er Brendan (.) and it erm (1s) means (1s) I think the preacher or er (1s)something along that line (..), I'm not too sure about the actual meaning but (..) °I like my name°	
85	Jessica	ah sorry >so I got it wrong so< Brendan is your first name (0.5s) and Simon is your surname (1s) right?	
86	Brendan	er yup that's correct	
87	silence	(9s)	Jessica: sorry
88	Jessica	next?	
89	silence	(15s)	
90	Brendan	°are you all there y'all there°	
91	silence	(4s)	
92	Jessica	Ok (you're) being shy (..) we we'll go round ok erm (..) Mohammed? does your name have a meaning?	

There are various strategies that the facilitators use to select speakers. At times they orient to aspects of their transportable identities. For instance in Turn 144 below (Table 7.5), Ranà orients to the identity category of gender, having noted that those who had not yet spoken were the female participants, as she says "I want to hear more about our ladies Fadela and Deni...", calling on them to participate.

Table 7.5. Session 1, Turns 144-145

Turn	Speaker	Audio	Text chat
144	Ranà	Oh thank you Alef very much for participating, what about our ladies I want to hear more about our ladies Fadela and Deni I want to know more from you?	
145	silence		Jessica: Ranà: let's hear more from our ladies Jessica: :-)

At other times they make explicit observations on the group dynamics in the session and seek to bring in voices and perspectives that have not yet been heard, as in the example below (Table 7.6), which again is from the first session. The co-facilitators share the responsibility of ensuring that all participants have the opportunity to make themselves heard and strategically use the different modes of communication available to encourage participation, reinforcing the spoken word through use of text and orienting to different aspects of participants' identities in order to do this in a non-threatening way. In the extract below one of the participants, Alef, also encourages other voices as he uses the text chat to reinforce the facilitator's encouragement. It takes some time, but after 13 seconds of silence, Jack indeed does respond, acknowledging the 'pressure' on him to do so, and expressing a degree of discomfort both with the topic being discussed and also the technology.

The facilitators are thus far the 'experts' in this community of practice as regards communication in this new online space, guiding the participant-novices as they negotiate the constraints of the technology as well as their engagement in dialogue about difficult issues in this new context where they are not yet familiar with one another. In terms of the relationality principle, when facilitators take on the initiator and orchestrator identity as in the extracts discussed above, the participants align to the identity of participant as obedient executor of facilitator instructions. There is an imbalance in terms of power relations, with the facilitators wielding the authority to initiate interactions, establish topics and decide who is next to speak.

Table 7.6. Session 1, Turns 244-246

Turn	Speaker	Audio	Text chat
244	Jessica	(5s) ok so the discussion is he he getting strong but I can notice it's seeming (..) a little bit one sided (2s) erm erm ( ) Egypt and we haven't heard anybody from 'hh the other side erm and we'll talk maybe about labels later does anyone have anything to say Jack Brendan Deni	Thamena: yes
			Alef: com on JACK :D
			JACK
245	silence	(13s)	
246	Jack	ok er I guess I'll talk for a little bit (2s) since I got pressured into it 'hh erm yeah I mean I don't stand ok i'll talk slower 'hh so: I don't exactly think that (.) the US did everything right obviously cause I mean it yeah I mean we didn't do everything the proper way and er er (°gosh I'm trying to think°) erm yeah I mean I don't know: what exactly I'm supposed to say I mean I think it's good that we're trying to help I just don't know (1s) what exactly we are supposed to do: (1s) beacause I mean er yeah I'm on the other side I'm um on the outside looking in so erm it's not for me to say like OH oh take I don't know how to explain this °I'm tired° aah: yeah I mean so it's kinda hard for me to (..) say what I've said is in the little box now erm (3s) but yeah I mean (2s) it's hard for me to speak about the government with the cat in front of my computer urm (3s) yeah I'm gonna (5s) he: ho yeah erm	Jessica: slowly please :)
			Jessica: I don't exactly think the US did everything right obviously
			Jessica: the proper way
			Jessica: Jack: don't know what to say
			Jessica: I don't know what exactly we are supposed to do
			Jessica: I'm on the other side, the outside looking in
			Jessica: so it's hard for me to say
			Jessica: it's hard to speak about teh government with teh cat

These interactions follow what has been identified as the most common interaction pattern in the classroom, *initiation-response-feedback* (Richards, 2006), with the facilitators Rană and Jessica taking on a role similar to that of the teacher. This is a familiar pattern to many of the participants perhaps, and offers a sense of safety and comfort, but does not lead to the depth of interactions and understanding that the programme aims for. As mentioned previously, the ultimate aim is for participants to take ownership of the dialogue process, to initiate the interactions themselves, and to delve deeper into issues which are of interest to them.

Each of the two hour sessions that were analysed in this study had parts that were characterised by this *initiation-response-feedback* pattern of interaction, but as the programme progressed there were some changes. In the first session the facilitators' floor time, in particular Jessica who had a stronger Internet connection and was present throughout the session, exceeded by far that of the participants. In fact, the two facilitators spoke more between them than the sum of the participants.

In the final session, the facilitators still initiate interactions and orchestrate the turn-taking, but their voice is no longer so dominant in terms of floor time. As participants become familiar with one another, the situated environment, and the technology mediating their sessions, they take ownership of the dialogue process. Their voices become stronger and the range of discourse identities they take on broadens. They are not only respondents but, as we will see in the following chapter, they initiate dialogue, they align, but also disalign, to one another, sometimes challenging the assumptions underlying one another's questions and affirmations. The facilitators do not disappear, but continue to orchestrate the interactions in less visible ways.

7.4. How did the facilitator identity evolve?

In the first session, much of the facilitator time was spent dealing with technical issues and, initially, orchestrating the interaction as participants became familiar with the turn-taking dynamics, the technology, and the group. These issues remained throughout the sessions, but as participants engaged in deeper interactions, the facilitators oriented to the identity of summariser and/or prober, pulling together the points of view which had been expressed, and adding an additional opportunity for listening and understanding. This can support the group in digging deeper into the conversation.

7.4.1. Summariser

In the extract below, we see Jessica (Table 7.7, Turn 250) orient to the situated identity of facilitator-summariser as she brings together various interventions and viewpoints expressed by the participants regarding the role of the US in the Middle East.

Table 7.7. Session 1, Turns 250-252

Turn	Speaker	Audio	Text chat
250	Jessica	ok so erm: I'm gonn Alef and Thamena talked a little bit about erm how erm even aid erm is very often carried out with interests in mind erm this is summarising the argument no and that er m intervention 'hh (..) talking about military intervention but also that kind of occupying or perhaps we can talk about hegemonising isn't just military it's also cultural in relation to food and er other aspects 'hh erm: Deni and Jack talking from the other side or from the outside looking in said that erm (2s) obviously it's not erm not everybody agrees with what the government does so erm they are erm they are speaking for doesn't mean they necessarily agree with what the government does (..) and erm 'hh they recognise that it's a complex situation that erm: they're expected to step in somehow but it's difficult to know how to step in and that erm (3s) 'hh very often there are interests does anybody else? (..) have something to say?	
251	silence	(9s)	

| 252 | Mohammed | yes can I ask something please I want to comment on what Alef had said about er being er developing countries and that we can help each other (..) 'hh what I want to say is that for how long do we really say er ( ) for how long do we say er developing countries we got money we got sciences we got everything er that developed countries have but er that is the only thing that we don't have is how er we use this resources (.) to be developed countries and I think the only solution is by er helping each other er (2s) I mean the Arab countries (..) thank you | Jessica: Mohammed: wants some comments on what Alef said about Tunisia being a developing a country |

Jessica explicitly indexes this identity as she says "this is summarising the argument" and she reiterates some of the words used by Thamena, such as 'military intervention' and 'occupying' and introduces her own interpretation with the term 'hegemonising' ("or perhaps we can talk about hegemonising isn't just military it's also cultural in relation to food and er other aspects 'hh erm"). She incorporates Jack and Deni's words, "talking from the other side or from the outside looking in", and acknowledges their recognition of the complexity of the situation and their perceived expectations of others as regards the US role. She closes her turn by orienting to the facilitator-orchestrator identity as she elicits any further interventions.

Another example of summarising comes from close to the end of the first session. Jessica returns to some key points that were raised in the dialogue in order to bring the participants to the topic of language and the categories they use. This is an activity that had been planned by the facilitators, as she had mentioned it previously in the session, and it aims to foster critical awareness. She is not 'teaching' them what is right and wrong, but rather trying to support them in establishing a shared language for the group that they feel comfortable with. The previous discussion highlighted the need for this as the participants themselves had initiated a discussion on terminology, in particular the use of the contentious terms 'help' and 'developing country' as Mohammed pointed out in Turn 252. Jessica indexes the group identity several times in her turn (264, Table 7.8), making reference to their shared goals and future activities "in the group discussions we're going to be talking about". She refers back to some of the terms that have already been used in that session – which constitutes the group's 'shared history'. In this turn she thus reinforces the community identity and the actions that the group will be engaging in, authenticating the group (Bucholtz & Hall, 2005, p. 598), making reference also to the emerging and imagined identity of the group.

Table 7.8. Session 1, Turn 264

Turn	Speaker	Audio	Text chat
264	Jessica	I don't know if Fadela wanted to say something I just wanted to summarise (..) erm or em raise the issues that a few of you mentioned (..) because of (..) important (3s) the whole issue of defining, no? maybe ( ) need to decide on the kind of labels we're going to use because as (..) umm (..) 'hh (2s) Alef said (...) that we're umm: (4s) there's so much diversity within the (.) what we call you know the Middle East or the Arab world or Arab countries 'hh (..) just as there is within Europe or within the United States so it's it's difficult to make generalisations (.) but it's also important (.) to come up with definitions that we're happy with because (...) in the group discussions we're going to be talking about a lot about a lot of these issues, ok, umm also words that are very loaded (.) like (.) 'help' who's in a position to help somebody? what is a developing country? so Alef (.) you said Tunisia is a developing country (.) would everybody agree with that? umm language has a lot of what to do with what ( ) to discuss (..) think about the labels that we're going to be using and that we're all going to be happy with (.) because (2s) it makes the conversation very difficult (.) if we're using words that erm (.) that are contentious (.) that people don't agree with 'hh (1s) so how how about some definitions (...) like the West (.) and the Arab and Muslim wo:rld (.) what would you be happy with	

Mirroring and summarising are indeed key strategies for facilitators which their training prepares them for, though as can be seen in the extracts above, it is not easy for a beginner facilitator to do this clearly. It is important that facilitators ask participants to correct them if they have misinterpreted what they said. Summarising is used in order to make sure that all group participants understand what has been said, particularly in long conversations when a lot of ideas emerge. It is also a way of helping participants feel listened to, and returning to key points.

7.4.2. Reframing

Another strategy that the facilitators used on several occasions was reframing, that is shifting the perspective of a discussion from, for example, the personal to the political, or from a specific context to a broader context, or shifting from the past to the future.

The extract below (Table 7.9) comes from the third session after an intense exchange between the participants about the situation in Palestine on a very personal level as they talk about the impact of Israeli occupation on their daily lives.

Table 7.9. Session 3, Turns 259-262

Turn	Speaker	Audio	Text chat
259	Jessica	(3s) erm to to go back to er ok he he we only got as far as two words in our word associations activity which was supposed to (.) lead on 'hh but I think maybe now erm I think it's he time he to go on to a broader discussion to relate this issue because some writers have 'hh (2s) erm (4s) mm say that the Palestine Israel issue is one of the: erm (3s) relationships between the west:ern world and Arab and Muslim world erm (2s) first of all can I ask you can you erm (2s) can you ASK can I ask if you think there IS a conflict between the western world and the Arab and Muslim world (2s) can you just type yes or no if you think there is some kind of 'hh conflict in the relationship between (2s) < the two sides > [air quotes gesture] 'hh	

260	silence	(37s)	Ranà: acn u tell if there is aa conflice between muslim and west?
			Kate: yes and no
			Jack: Yes
			Denise: yes
			Jessica: Is there a conflict between the "west" and the "Arab and Muslim world"?
			Brendan: yes, unfortunatel
			Fadela: not direct one
261	Jessica	(4s) and I was just wondering about erm how related you think the Arab the Israel Palestinian issue is to this greater conflict 'hh erm for example Kofi Annan said that resolving this major issue would help relations I don't know if you think that's true Fadela you said that's not a direct 'hh (2s) conflict	
262	silence		Mohammed: not for surenes

Jessica links the exchange they have had to a broader discussion on the 'nature of the relationship' between 'western societies' and 'predominantly Muslim societies'. She thus reframes the issue, which leads to a shift from a very personal, emotional tone to a more structured, rational discussion which she and Ranà lead. There are many false starts and hesitations in Jessica's turn as she sets up the activity, but she finally starts this new discussion, orienting to the multimodal affordances of the platform as she asks the participants to respond to her question through the text mode.

This (somewhat inarticulate) reframing leads to a different kind of discussion which focusses more on the political level, redressing participation imbalances by allowing those that do not have personal experience, but may have some academic or political knowledge, to have a voice.

Reframing is, like mirroring and summarising, one of the active listening tools that facilitators are trained to use in order to facilitate online dialogue. It allows the facilitator to move the conversation forward – in this case by connecting it to a larger theme, but there are many ways of reframing. It is a strategy that can also be used to connect people with conflicting views, or to highlight differences between the perspectives that are coming into the conversation. It is valuable in creating awareness in dialogue by drawing attention to, and even naming the frames that are being used and those which may be missing. It relates to power dynamics in that it is often who starts the discussion that establishes the frame that is being used and the way the discussion of a topic is approached (Soliya, 2010). Reframing issues allows for shifts in power dynamics within the dialogue group. Awareness of framing is also an important aspect of critical media literacy, for frames "organize the world both for journalists who report it and, in some important degree, for us who rely on their reports" (Gitlin, 1980, p. 7).

7.5. Reflective practitioner

Another essential identity orientation of the facilitator is that of the reflective practitioner, who with the group reflects on the dialogue process, usually in the final 'closing round' of the sessions. Reflections on the dialogue process are fundamental (Andreotti, 2005; Greenwood, 2005; Lederach, 1995; Saunders, 1999) as they allow the participants to reflect on what they have learnt and share how they are feeling. It also encourages participants to take responsibility for the group process by making it explicit and encouraging them to think how they would like to move forward and also better their dialogue and communication (Soliya, 2010). Furthermore, it provides valuable feedback for the facilitators themselves on how they are performing and supporting the group.

As analysis of the closing rounds of each of the three sessions showed, this activity allows group members to re-align to one another after having engaged in distinction and even made negative evaluations of each others' positionings (Bucholtz & Hall, 2005).

At the end of the first session, Jessica makes observations on the progress that the group has made in this single session (Table 7.10). Despite the technical issues which she and Ranà had been grappling with (or perhaps in part due to them) the participants had talked about East-West relations which, according to the curriculum, should be addressed in later weeks, when the group has established trust. Jessica asks them to reflect on what they liked and did not like about the session or that they had learnt (questions from the 'Online Curriculum').

Table 7.10. Session 1, Turn 302

Turn	Speaker	Audio	Text chat
302	Jessica	well guys erm he he the discussion has really got (.) moving on I think we have (1s) dealt with a lot of things this week 'hh (...) ok so just erm (1s) a quick closing round ok I want erm each person to say 'hh something that they erm that they liked ( ) didn't like about today's session (2s) ok or something that you liked or something that you learnt in today's session	

The shift from a focus on distinction and differences to adequation and shared identities, from seriousness to celebration lightens the tone of the final interactions and moves the focus to cohesion, a strong indicator of community (Hauck, Galley, & Warnecke, 2016). The extract below comes from the end of the third session as the participants reflect on what they learnt through their interaction and exchange which had been particularly intense as the Palestine Israel conflict was discussed. In Turn 387 (Table 7.11), Fadela acknowledges the seriousness of the discussions but shifts her positioning and orients to the group in a different way, announcing she has news. She then indexes the identity she shares with the group – that of being a student as she reminds them that she will soon be graduating and shares the photo of her graduation attire. The group identity and realignment is reinforced through the phatic communication expressed through text chat mode as participants congratulate Fadela.

In this case, the orientation to group cohesion was indexed and brought into play by a participant and not a facilitator. This shift in tone eases the tension which may have emerged during the session and allows the participants to realign. The initiation of the closing round, an institutional activity, sets the ground for this shift which is why it is a fundamental part of dialogue practices in the fields of intergroup relations, conflict transformation, and other related fields (Andreotti, 2005; Saunders, 1999).

Table 7.11. Session 3, Turns 383-389

Turn	Speaker	Audio	Text chat
383	Brendan	I learnt that the: feelings or associations between Arabs and Israelis is stronger than ever or just as strong as when the conflict apparently started	
384	silence	(6s)	
385	Ranà	thanks Brendan Fadela? would you please tell us if er you have learnt ( ) new things and what er how you felt today while er our discussion?	Jessica: Brendan. learnt that feelings between Arabs and iIsraelis is strong
386	silence	(3s)	Jessica: maybe as strong as when conflict started
387	Fadela	I think that the discussion today was he serious he 'hh somehow and I I knew that before but I'm sure now that we have individual differences (.) between people of the sa:me country so we cannot judge people by (..) the er (.) the er few people who represent them (1s) so (1s) we have to look (1s) er deeper: we have to have a deeper vision into societies 'hh to: know to differentiate between the right and the wrong 'hh (..) and to have (a side) with the right 'hh (°for sure°) and I want to tell you something 'hh and er er it was er really interesting today 'hh and I want to share something ( ) I have told you before 'hh I will be graduating this: yea >this semester< 'hh (..) and er I got something to ( ) he he graduation: dress 'hh so I want to show to you the dress he he [shows photo of her with mortar board on head] (5s) erm thank you (6s)	Jessica: Fadela: I think discussion today was serious somehow Jessica: Fadela: I knew before, and confirmed that peole inside societies have different opinions Jessica: Fadela- will be graduating today Jessica: this is her graduation dress Brendan: congratulations Thamena: congratsss
388	Fadela	(10s)	Jessica: congratulations!! Denise: congrats!

389	Ranà	(11s) well congratulations Fadela for your graduation we are (.) happy that you shared this with us it's a great picture and thank you for sharing 'hh and as you see Jessica is asking you to er publish your er photo on our blog via Soliya ( ) or the Facebook group if you find it? then er let's hear now from Doja Doja can you go ahead please?	Fadela: thxxxxxxxxxxx
			Mohammed: cogratulations Fadela
			Jessica: Can you post the picture to us in your blog or facebook!

7.6. Tensions in the facilitator identities

7.6.1. Silence

There was a tension in the facilitator's role of orchestrator, linked to their comfort with silence. Throughout the sessions, there were occasions when silences lasted for several minutes, not just seconds. As highlighted at various points of the analysis, this is much longer than silences identified in face to face interactions in studies which analyse face to face interactions adopting conversation analysis, in which microseconds are counted. There has been a tendency to perceive silence as indicating lack of mutual rapport or indexing lower cognitive or indeed language abilities in mainstream European and American cultures (Jaworski, 1993; Li, 2001). Although analysing the different types of silence was beyond the scope of this study, different explanations for silence were found: technical issues, lack of familiarity with turn taking mechanisms, and resistance to the topic being discussed. However, silence also seemed to serve as 'think time' and preparing to speak in silence allows time for reflection and can facilitate more meaningful interactions. Silent 'wait-time' has been found to increase the number and quality of unsolicited responses (Li, 2001) in the classroom.

Finding the right balance between giving the interactants time to think of their responses and follow up questions is perhaps one of the most difficult tasks for facilitators, as they seek to encourage the group to 'take ownership' of the process, but also do not want them to disengage due to prolonged silences. Yet intervening too often will prevent the participants from taking control of the dialogue. This tension was visible in many instances of the sessions.

7.6.2. Neutrality and multipartiality

Facilitators in the Soliya Connect Program are expected not to contribute their views to the dialogues, but to be multipartial (Soliya, 2010), in the sense that they should be curious about and pay attention to all perspectives and even seek to bring in those which may not be presented in the dialogue, for example by playing devil's advocate. It is not easy to be multipartial and facilitators need training, self-observation, and reflexivity, as well as supervision, time, and practice,, to acquire these skills. There is a risk that facilitators can cause more harm than good, hence the importance of the training and supervision of facilitators. Agbaria and Cohen (2000) suggest that facilitators that "encounter experiences with groups in conflict" (p. 8) should themselves have gone through such experiences and dealt with issues of power as participants in such groups or issues pertaining to their own identity and the dynamics of power relations in their own lives.

This neutrality and multipartiality can represent a tension for facilitators, certainly in my experience as a facilitator I have often felt and reflected on this, as have others (Bali, 2014). However, I have come to the understanding that being neutral when performing the identity of facilitator does not mean that one cannot have political and/or religious beliefs. Facilitating can be seen as orienting to a situated identity in which these beliefs are temporarily suspended, or not explicitly indexed whilst serving the needs of a group and a larger 'cause'. Supporting groups in negotiation and working with them so they frame their interests in such a way that 'others' can effectively respond can be seen as a way of pursuing the same goal of social justice (Burgess, 2005). It is clear, however, that before and whilst 'doing being a facilitator', these beliefs and allegiances should not be visible to the participants in the dialogue groups.

7.7. Imagined identities

As mentioned in Chapter 5, the facilitators are key to this model of virtual exchange; without them the programme could not exist. Most of the facilitators are volunteer facilitators who have been through the Connect Program themselves and have continued to engage with Soliya through facilitation. They thus represent, in some ways, the 'imagined identity' that the Soliya Connect Program prefigures for participants. In focus groups with facilitators in a more recent study[2], I have been exploring the driving force behind facilitators' commitment to the Soliya Connect Program, as they undertake to facilitating the same group, at the same time, for two hour sessions over eight consecutive weeks. There is also a considerable amount of preparation and communication with co-facilitators and participants in between sessions.

What many of the facilitators responded was what they learn from each round of facilitation that they do. Every group is different and has their own dynamics, hence every group presents different challenges in terms of facilitation, which makes it an opportunity for learning. As this facilitator from Egypt reported: "I feel like I am developing my skills each time I have a different challenge and I try just to develop myself as a facilitator and let them get the best out of this experience". It is also the new knowledge that the facilitators engage with as they listen to their group's dialogue and participants' experiences which offers them learning opportunities. An additional factor is the support which they receive from the community of facilitators and coaches, and the "feeling part of a global community, being around people from different countries".

Facilitators also reported applying the skills that they developed through this experience to other spheres of their life, for example their relationships with friends, their work contexts, and family.

> "I think it's a valuable skill in life to be able to be a good participant in dialogue and improve relations and in negotiations and to be able also to be a positive force within any dialogue on a day to day basis so it's a skill which is valuable and I'm liking it, I enjoy it and I feel comfortable doing it" (Facilitator, Netherlands).

2. This research/activity is being carried out under a contract with the Education, Audiovisual and Culture Executive Agency financed by the Union's budget. The opinions expressed are those of the contractor only and do not represent the contracting authority's official position.

Many of the facilitators said they felt they were making a difference, and that is what keeps them facilitating. Several of them talked about experiencing transformation themselves when they had been participants which is what led them to facilitation. As facilitators, they report the pleasure in witnessing this change in some of the participants, it is this tangible impact that drives them.

> "So why I facilitate is because I see the change and I'm passionate about intercultural dialogue I want... that there is more peace and understanding between people... I feel I'm making a difference for three years now and I see the difference at the end of the semester with my groups... and really I feel global, I feel like I'm a citizen of the world, I feel how the world is connected and how small it is and I like helping others to have that amazing wonderful feeling that makes me happy at least, and yeah this feeling of connection" (Facilitator, Sweden).

> "I'm on my senior year in university now and I have a very busy schedule I'm not going to sign up for second semester but then at the end I saw it come to me... it's really great when you can be part of a change of someone else and at the same time you feel the change in your life" (Facilitator, Morocco).

Participant identities

In the previous chapter, I explored the facilitator identities within this situated context, but in this chapter I turn to the participant identities. While the facilitators focussed on faciliating the dialogue process and maintained their institutional role, participants were free to orient to a wider range of transportable identities, that is those markers of identity that are not situation-dependent (as in facilitator and participant), but rather can be transported from one situation to another – for example national identities, gender, social class, professions, etc. These may or may not become relevant in the interactions, it depends whether they are oriented to by the participants.

As discussed in Chapter 5, on the website and in the design of the educational programme Soliya makes use of the labels/categories 'Western societies' and 'predominantly Muslim societies', reproducing dominant and often polarising media discourses and framing the 'relationship' as a problem between 'one side' and 'the other'. These categories, like most categories, are problematic for they reduce differences to single traits, as if these societies were completely homogeneous. Yet using these categories strategically can open a space for dialogue and create understanding between participants as it allows for an analytical stance through which participants can begin to unpack categories, and how they are used.

In Chapter 6, when exploring mediation, we saw how in their asynchronous identities as expressed through their blog posts, some of the participants made relevant their identities as students, as English language learners, as members of certain nation states, and/or smaller community contexts. However, there was hardly any interaction with their peers or engagement in relations of similarity or difference, authentication, or delegitimisation, for these blog posts were largely monologic and uni-directional. They were written before the participants started their dialogue sessions and they were projecting their identities into an unknown space almost. In the synchronous interactions however, as we shall see in this chapter, relations did emerge as participants oriented to aspects of one another's identities, showing alignment but also disalignment to one another. Orientations to identities were more fluid and dynamic, influencing their participation in the interactions in several ways.

8.1. English learners or users? "I think my English capability is enough"

Several of the participants in this group had made relevant their identity as learners of English in their blog posts – by suggesting, for example, that they wanted to improve their language through participation in this programme or that they were majoring in English language studies. Also, in the first session, as they introduced themselves, some of the participants made this identity relevant. However, there are a couple of instances in the sessions when the facilitators implicitly cast some of the participants into the category of English learner, but they resist this categorisation.

In session 3 (Table 8.1), for example, after a long exchange on a difficult issue, R_anà suggests that if participants feel they can express themselves better in their 'own native language' it is not a problem. In Turn 333, there is silence as Jessica summarises Ranà's words in the transcription and adds that Ranà will translate for them. This offer could be seen to imply a negative evaluation of participants' language competence, and the emoticon at the end of Jessica's turn can be seen as an attempt to mitigate this potential face threat.

There is an extended silence after this turn, and perhaps again addressing the possible implication of her words, that she and Ranà are suggesting some of the Arabic speakers of the group are not effective communicators, Jessica adds a line of text asking Ranà if she will also translate Filipino, with three question marks that hint at the intended playfulness of her words. In the video we see Kate smiling, but she does not take the floor. Ranà orients to the category of

Filipino speaker (Turn 334) and addresses Kate directly saying she would love to learn Filipino, laughing and smiling. Kate seems to align to this and also smiles, but through the text chat she resists being cast into the category of non-proficient English speaker in need of support, or indeed the category of 'teacher of Filipino' as she types "it's okay" then makes specific reference to her English competence being adequate. Just before Kate's response, a line of text typed by Jessica appears with just the word 'joking' written, suggesting she realises the potential face threat that her words presented to Kate.

Table 8.1. Session 3, Turns 332-338

Turn	Speaker	Audio	Text chat
332	Rana	well er ( ) for you all guys if anyone feels er any time that he better he feels better 'hh to speak on his ow:n er native language please go ahead and don't worry about it we will handle: every thing er but if you thought that you can express better in your own language.	
333	silence	(30s)	Jessica: Rana: if you want to speak in your own language that's fine
			Jessica: Rana will translate :-)
			Jessica: Filippino too Rana???
334	Rana	well Kate I would love to learn Filippino he he we (will leave you with this task though)	
335	silence	(24s)	Kate: it's okay
			Jessica: joking
			Kate: I think my english capability is en=ough
336	Jessica	hh hh I just want to say that erm everyone's English is great 'hh and erm I think it's really good (1.5s) that we're managing to have this discussion. 'hh (1s) and a lot of people whose language (..) it isn't their first language (3s) erm: so well done everyone (1s) good (..) keep going hh (4s)	
337	silence	(25s)	

| 338 | Jessica | ok then let me ask Doja Doja is that right Doja said it it's erm (..) it's ourselves it's a personal thing it's it's people 'h that cause conflict and tension 'hh so: (2s) you don't think governments are responsible either? or historic factors or (3s) multinationals as well economic interests? which aren't always necessarily related to governments? | |

Jessica then takes the floor (Turn 336) to offer clarification and orients to those for whom English is **not** their main language, that is those whose face may have been threatened by the assumption underlying the offer to support through translation. Jessica thus makes language proficiency relevant, albeit in a positive way as she compliments them on their English. However, this can also be seen to reinforce a power differential in that it categorises her as an 'expert' with the authority to assess their competence, and consequently the participants as 'non-experts'. Her words highlight the fact that the interactions are taking place in what is a foreign or second/third language for the majority of participants and recognise the additional effort that may be required of 'non-experts', but the participants seem to resist this categorisation as there is a long silence after Jessica's turn, without even comments in the text chat.

After 25 seconds of silence, Jessica takes the floor once again (Turn 338) and returns to the point of discussion before this brief interlude regarding language use. She orients to Doja's previous turn regarding people causing conflict rather than religions. As she nominates Doja as next speaker, she aligns to her own identity as non-expert in pronunciation of Arabic names, and asks Doja if she is pronouncing her name correctly (since previously in this session Doja had corrected her pronunciation), categorising Doja as expert, in what can be seen as a form of redressive action, that 'gives face' to the addressee (Brown & Levinson, 1987).

English language proficiency is topicalised once again at the beginning of the final session when Jessica seeks to start a discussion on the use of English in this programme (Table 8.2, Turn 81).

Table 8.2. Session 7, Turns 81-88

Turn	Speaker	Audio	Text chat
81	Jessica	ok then erm I did have a question for erm everybody 'hh (1s) ( ) working in English and whose language isn't English (1s) did you have any trouble ? with language? how do you <u>feel</u> (1s) how do you feel (1s) about using English (1s) as a language to communicate in the Soliya sessions and for making the video 'hh erm do you like it ? er do you have problems with it (..) are there any issues	
82	silence	(7s)	
83	Mohammed	((background noise people talking))	
84	Mohammed	hmm hm sorry for that but I want to say er that er concerning the English language er we er I think it was quite difficult er but er you know (1s) thanks to you (1s) it was er quite easy you: work hard to: facilitate our job here (1s) so thank you 'hh er about the video project as we said er the last session er the material wasn't quite enough (1s) so we did our best	Jessica: Fran: how do you feel about using English as a language in this program Jessica: and for video project Jessica: are you happy with it?
85	silence	(7s)	Jessica: Mohammed: found it difficult at times, but facs made it easier :-)
86	Mohammed	((lots of background noise))	Rànà: most welcome Mohammed Jessica: not enough materials for video project
87	silence	(26s)	Jessica: go Jack Mohammed: sorry for that
88	Jessica	Nobody else? about the fact that do you see English the spread of English erm as a tool for spreading western values 'hh for spreading western ideas and concepts? or do you see it as a neutral language (..) I'm just wondering (2s)	

In asking the question, Jessica explicitly orients to those "whose language isn't English", the majority of participants in this setting. Jessica's framing of the question explicitly excludes Jack and Deni, the two American participants present, and it casts the other participants into the category of 'non-native speakers' of English. In terms of Bucholtz and Hall's (2005) principle of indexicality discussed in Chapter 3, she is linking English to the 'native speaker' and authenticating the common sense assumption that English 'belongs' to native speakers. However, she could have framed the discussion differently, for example in terms of plurilingualism, or the challenges of communicating in online transcultural contexts such as this one. In this way the discussion would have included all participants and the linguistic resources of the group would have been highlighted rather than the assumptions of inadequacy that she unwittingly alluded to.

There is a long pause after the question, Mohammed has the floor for 25s (probably due to a technical glitch) before responding. He orients to the category of 'non-expert' English user saying he thought participation was difficult. Mohammed was actually the participant who most frequently oriented to the text chat to request repetition or clarification from facilitators. He also makes relevant the situated identity of the facilitators and their role in supporting understanding and communication. However, none of the other participants take the floor after Mohammed, suggesting a resistance to being cast into the category of non-expert speaker.

Unlike language classrooms where L2 proficiency is a public matter that is topicalised and discussed, L2 proficiency is essentially a private matter that is not alluded to or topicalised in some contexts. Firth (2009), for example, found that in 'lingua franca workplace settings' interactants "disavow any intimations of 'learner' status" (p. 127), and artfully deflect attention from and circumvent potential or actual language encoding difficulties. The shared space of Soliya could be seen to have similar characteristics as there are few instances when language proficiency is made relevant. On the many occasions when there are dysfluencies, these are dealt with by participants and facilitators implicitly, with a focus on the meaning of the message rather than correctness of form.

In this extract, however, Jessica does not deflect attention away from the topic of language but rather makes more explicit what she was alluding to. Jessica reframes the discussion on participants' feelings as regards the use of English within a framework of 'linguistic imperialism', indexing the work of Phillipson (1992) and the conceptualisation of the spread of English as a deliberate effort by the Anglosphere to sustain political and economic dominance while concealing "the fact that the use of English serves the interests of some much better than others" (Phillipson, 2000, p. 89). This is in line with arguments that Fadela and Thamena had made in a previous session as regards the US being a 'dominant culture'. Now, in the final session, Jessica asks if they consider English as a neutral language, but unlike their previous self-initiated discussion of dominant cultures, they do not orient to the question.

Finally, after a long pause of 30 seconds, Fadela orients to Jessica's question (Table 8.3, Turn 90). She first of all categorises herself as an English user, who feels comfortable speaking English. The audio quality makes it difficult to understand everything she is saying, but later in her turn she implicitly indexes her English learner identity as she makes relevant the notion of proficiency when she says she feels she is improving her language. There is a duality here, she identifies as an English user, but to align with the facilitator's question and the identity it has cast her into, she also orients to the language learner identity.

Table 8.3. Session 7, Turns 90-94

Turn	Speaker	Audio	Text chat
90	Fadela	((very tiny sound)) I see it as a very ( ) I don't know ( ) talking about myself using the English language here 'hh is er I feel very very 'hh comfortable to speak English 'hh in front of you ( ) because I have ( ) he he but it's a ( ) to use English and er after I finish every session I go home and I ( ) hehh hehh the next day 'hh and er I'm really happy for that because I er I feel that I'm improving (..) my language and also 'hh I (can speak confidently) and (we) will see that er my comments about you in the ( ) in the sessions that I wrote (4s)	Jessica: Fadela: this is last session, go ahead guys Jessica: Fadela: feels comfortable speaking English Jessica: after session will go home and continue speaking English - right?

91	Silence	(182s) [message appears on screen at one point saying server is disconnected S7P2_ lostconnection – Tech issues are probably due to Jessica and Ranà trying to set up poll as in plan and as stated at the beginning of the session]	Jessica: is happy about using English
92	Mohammed	Hey guys is it a minute of silence?	
93	silence	(7s)	
94	Mohammed	( ) is a neutral language er you have to learn it er if you want to have a great job er (2s) it's different here you can't speak English er around you or with other people ((interference)) because many of them don't er know er the English language er and it's difficult because er people find it difficult to learn English and er any other language 'hh er but I	

After Fadela's turn there is a long silence (over three minutes), due in part to technical issues, broken by Mohammed who takes the floor and makes relevant this silence, attempting to ease the tension by using irony "hey guys is it a minute of silence?" (Turn 92). Following further lack of reaction, after eight seconds he orients to Jessica's question, categorising himself as an English learner for whom English is a requirement in order to have a good job. He highlights the difference between his context and Fadela's, saying it is difficult to speak English with others as most people do not know English but he says, at the beginning of his turn, that he sees English as a neutral language. Mohammed's turn is interesting for he stated that he needs English for a job, thus aligning himself with the neoliberal cosmopolitanism identified by Camicia and Franklin (2010, as discussed in Chapter 4) and the neoliberal agenda often associated with English as a foreign language. At the same time he says he feels that English is neutral. Through the sessions the participants have engaged with and critiqued many 'macrolevel' assumptions linked to cultures but they perhaps have not yet reached a level of interrogation that allows them to see how language use is also a socio-political positioning.

These extracts highlight the Soliya participants' resistance to the categorisation of 'non-expert' speakers of the English language, and to the topicalisation of language proficiency in the interactions. This topicalisation excluded the American participants from the interaction, and was clearly not seen as relevant to the shared goals of the group. As mentioned in Chapter 1, this virtual exchange is not a foreign language telecollaboration exchange where the aim is for participants to improve their language proficiency and intercultural awareness, but the aims are, as the facilitators made relevant in Session 1, to foster empathy and respect for diverse views and to build positive relationships of respect with others, to foster critical awareness and thinking, and the ability to engage in constructive dialogue. The fact that Fadela, Mohammed, Thamena, Doja, and Maawa are students majoring in 'English', as they self-categorised themselves in Session 1 or in their blogs (Chapter 6), is not made relevant in the extracts above. This is clearly *not* perceived as a foreign language exchange for any of the participants, even for those who are students of applied English and may have initially approached it as such. This does not mean, however, that language learning was not taking place (Firth, 2009).

8.2. Othering: "for those er in our group in the Middle East"

There are several occasions in the interactions when the participants make their own and others' transportable identities relevant in the dialogue sessions. In the first session, after participants have introduced themselves and their motivations for taking part in the Connect Program, the facilitator asks if they have questions for one another. At this point one of the participants, Brendon (Table 8.4), formulates a question which he directs to "those in our group in the Middle East" and asks whether they are affected by recent events in their daily life. He does not explain exactly what events he is referring to (though as mentioned in the introduction the sessions took place in March 2011, at the height of the so-called 'Arab Spring') nor mention a specific country. He is orienting to the identities made relevant in the Soliya Connect Program website and implicitly positions himself as a 'Westerner' as the others as 'those in the Middle East'.

Table 8.4. Session 1, Turns 166-167

Turn	Speaker	Audio	Text chat
166	Jessica	Any questions? for for anybody in the group in particular? (3s)	
167	Brendan	Um: for those er in our group in the Middle East er what is it like on a (..) daily basis rather than like (..) forgetting all (political) or um: (1s) otherwise further like (..) implemented opinions like what is it like on a daily basis living there with all the events going on er if you're like directly affected by them or not (was wondering how that goes on) like on a daily basis	Jessica: What is it like on a dialy basis Jessica: for those of you in the Middle East, Brendan asks Jessica: Brendan: Are you directly affected by events?

Kate first of all asks for clarification and then aligns to this categorisation as she explains the situation in Qatar (Table 8.5). Though in a previous interaction she had spoken about her Filipino nationality, here she makes relevant her affiliation with Qatar as this authorises her to respond to Brendon. She uses the plural pronoun 'we' when referring to the situation of people in Qatar; "we want the country to be secure".

In following up, the facilitator R.anà explicitly calls on Alef and Mohammed to provide information about the situation, implicitly indexing their Tunisian and Egyptian identities by making reference to "more interesting and exciting details about what happened as you were in the middle of the events".

Alef and Mohammed also align to the identities that they have been cast into as they take the floor with little hesitation and take extended turns, each lasting several minutes. Alef begins by orienting to the identity of Tunisian as says "for me Tunisia is gaining security back ( ) these days 'hh er since we had a new … uu a new er (..) government […]". Mohammed also takes the floor and seeks to explain the situation in Egypt with an extended turn.

In terms of power dynamics and identities, what is significant is that this participant-initiated interaction in which participants' transportable identities were made relevant led to the first series of extended responses from some of the participants (Kate, Alef, and Mohammed). Brendan's question, which expressed an interest in the impact of the political situation on the daily lives of "those in the Middle East", and Rana's follow up call, positioned them not only as young people living in Qatar, Egypt, and Tunisia, but also as 'experts' and authorised them to take these extended turns and talk about aspects of their daily lives in their local contexts. Their increased agency in this exchange could also be considered as marking their investment in the group's shared goals which were expressed in the Motivations activity they had previously engaged in with the support of the facilitators, that is achieving greater understanding of 'the other' and what is happening in other parts of the world.

Table 8.5. Session 1, Turns 172-174

Turn	Speaker	Audio	Text chat
172	Kate	(2s) well (..) I guess now since Qatar is one of the last countries aside from the United Arab Emirates that (.) is not affected by the (1s) erm (protesting) going on around the Middle East erm today when I was going home from school we were on high security (..) erm like usually the police here in the cou in this country um don't carry (.) guns with them but today (..) we are on high alert because ( ) in this country about this protest going on around is very high (.) they're (3s) more (1s) they're er making the country more secure (2s) but regarding the basic needs and the relationship between other people 'hh it's pretty much the same (..) I mean it's not at all risky (..) it's just that we want er (1s) the country to be secure (.) cos (1s) since we won the bid in Qatar 2022 for the FIFA world cup (1s) they need to (as) err show that Qatar is a very secured country	Jessica: How's your daily life affected by tehe events Jessica: Kate: Qatar is one of the last countries which is not affected Jessica: by what is going on Jessica: Today going home from school was on high security Jessica: Usu the police here don't carry guns Jessica: but today they had guns Jessica: Kate: they're making the country more secure Jessica: regarding basic needspretty much the same, Jessica: not at all risky Jessica: want the country to be secure Jessica: because in Qatar
173	silence	(4s)	

174	Ranà	Thanks Kate so much I think Alef and Mohammed can give us more interesting and exciting details 'hh about what happened as you were in the middle of the events 'hh so I I I want to hear from both of them	Jessica: sorry missed last part
			Jessica: about 2022
			Jessica: ?
			Kate: since Qatar won the FIFA bid
			Jessica: Ranà. wants to hear from both

8.3. "We have Hilary Clinton coming tomorow to Tunisia"

The next excerpt (Table 8.6), which comes from the same initial session, shortly after the extract described above, is also of interest in terms of the principles of indexicality and relationality. The extract actually comes from the text chat which for several minutes became the main communication mode.

Table 8.6. Session 1

Alef: we have Hilary Clinton coming7 (6s)
Alef: tomorow to Tunisia (36s)
Alef: to meet Tunisian youth and officials (59s)
Alef: I'll be there in the meeting (5s)
Thamena: Oh really? (17s)
Mohammed: the meeting is about what? (5s)
Fadela: do u think that her visit will help? (19s)
Alef: Muhammed: I heard that no one in Egypt accepted to meet her? (21s)
Ranà: thats right alef (7s)
Ranà: :) (14s)
Mohammed: perhaps because its our problem (15s)
Mohammed: and we want to solve it ourselves (18s)
Mohammed: we need no help (12s)
Alef: JACK: what's the purpose of Clinton's visit to Tunisia and Egypt, now, in your opinion?

Alef positions himself as a Tunisian, who is going to meet Hillary Clinton the following day. The reaction from co-participants to his claim that Hillary

Clinton is coming to Tunisia is slow in coming, so he gradually provides more information in order to elicit a response or interest from his peers. However when he does obtain reactions from Mohammed and Fadela he does not align to the discourse identity of respondent that their questions cast him into, but rather takes on the discourse identity of initiator with a new question, orienting to Mohammed's Egyptian identity as he says he heard that no one in Egypt wanted to meet her. In terms of relationality, he is here orienting to difference in political orientations on a national level. Interestingly, Ranà, the facilitator, responds to Alef, making relevant her transportable identity of Egyptian rather than her institutional identity, which is one of the few occasions in which the facilitators do this. She then follows up her response with a smile emoticon, which could be seen to suggest alignment with Egyptians' political stance of not meeting Clinton, or could suggest a playful tone. It is Mohammed who then offers an explanation, orienting to his Egyptian identity, posing Clinton's visit as a problem and indexing undesired and unnecessary US interference. Alef orients to Mohammed's evaluative orientation of US foreign policy, but rather than directing his response to Mohammed, he indexes Jack's American identity by explicitly calling on him, using capital letters for emphasis, asking his opinion on the purpose of Clinton's visit to Tunisia.

This interaction subsequently shifts from text to the oral mode (see Table 8.7 below) with Jack responding to Alef's elicitation after a 19 second silence. Perhaps in part due to the implicit negative evaluations of Clinton's visit to Egypt, Jack (Turn 214) shows reluctance and insecurity in his response, first suggesting that his view is not important and then making excuses and apologising for not being informed on the topic. He could be seen as trying to 'disalign' himself from the readily available macro identity of 'uninformed American' as he offers many apologies and reasons for not following the news. Jack expresses empathy with how "you guys" might feel, thus authenticating the negative stance expressed by Mohammed towards US intervention ("I totally understand if you guys don't want her help") and possibly adequating to this viewpoint ("because some people tend to be nosey"). Implicit in his words is the assumption that the US's aim is to 'help' these countries and that these countries are in need of help, which was initially suggested by Fadela in her turn through the text chat ("do u think that her visit will help?").

Table 8.7. Turns 214-219

Turn	Speaker	Audio	Text chat
214	Jack	(>it's got nothing to do with how I think since nobody is really doing it with (question) it<) urm yeah uhh I uh honestly haven't been too up to date with what kind of like the recent things (...) so I mean I'm not exactly (.) su:re (..) >I've just been< so overloaded with final week last week a:nd (.) trying to get any sleep ( ) hh bu(h h h)t hh >[puts on funny voice] °I feel bad now°< uhm (2s) ye:ah hh (1s) >I don't know I know Clinton's been (.) trying to go (.) all over the place< and yeah I mean (.) >I totally understand that< uhm (..) yeah (3s) if (...) you guys don't want ( ) her help then (...) but yeah (...) because >some people tend to be nosey< and yeah (...) I dunno) (...) I'm gonna stop talking right now he he	
215	silence	(8s)	
216	Alef	Well Jack it's not that we (...) don't do not accept any help from the (2s) (...) United States or we consider like ( ) err (ms) Clinton is gonna gonna coming for .uhm. I dunno with bad intentions but it's er it's like as an anwer to the: (..) American .err (..) stand. before and after the revolution >that we went through to< ( ) err while we were getting killed and burnt by the prior er (5s) ( ) didn't show any err (2s) reaction, they (.) only showed concern about the situation in the Middle East (.) but (3s) they didn't do anything to stop (.) er the crimes that (7s) that we are er trying to form a new (life) in the region (...) that's it er I'm not sure if (4s) Mohammed from Egypt shares (...)	
217	Mohammed	°(I remember) I I I think that the only (1s) er (thing) (4s) er idea (...) of the American governement is concerned about the the oil (1s) (...) oil rich countries just to take their (3s) their wealth (8s) (now) er the United States governement has (avowed) to change many wrong er ideas here in er	
218	Silence	(11s)	Alef: too bad then, we have no oil in Tunisia :D lol
219	Mohammed	I'm (not) talking about er Tunisia but I'm talking about Libya about er	

After a short pause, Alef follows up on Jack's response (Turn 216). He does not challenge the assumption that the US should or intends to offer 'help'. He instead offers reasons for the negative stance towards the US, using the third person plural pronoun 'they' to refer to the US – so not equating Jack with the US government which the second person pronoun would have done.

This delicately constructed interaction could be seen as an example of mutual achievement of understanding, with participants seeking to align themselves as authentic participants in an intercultural community of practice in which 'big government' decisions do not include them. Although Alef indexes a negative evaluation of the US government which failed to react to events in the Middle East, in terms of the relationality principle discussed in the theoretical framework, he 'denaturalises' (Bucholtz & Hall, 2005) the assumption that all Americans are aligned with their government in his choice of the third person plural pronoun 'they', which excludes Jack from that categorisation.

Alef uses the first person plural 'we' to refer to the Middle East and North Africa, indexing a shared identity, at the same time showing caution in terms of representing all 'Middle Eastern participants' in the group by checking whether Mohammed aligns to this inclusive 'we' he has used ("that's it er I'm not sure if (4s) Mohammed from Egypt shares", Turn 216). Mohammed responds immediately (Turn 217), expressing a slightly diverging opinion – that the US is only interested in oil, maintaining a negative evaluation of them. Alef responds with a comment in the text chat (Turn 218), indexing the humorous tone he has used with a smiley face and 'lol'). This can be interpreted as a form of phatic communication in order to alleviate possible tensions that the discussion may be creating. Mohammed, however, does not orient to the humour and responds with clarification that he was referring to Libya, not Tunisia, perhaps interpreting Alef's comment as an attempt to delegitimise what he has said.

Later within the same session, as the participants are discussing the language they are to use in the sessions and the labels they feel comfortable using, Alef expresses disalignment and dissatisfaction with the label Middle East, stating preference for labels such as North African or Maghrebian if necessary, because he does not consider Tunisia as part of the Middle East or the Arab world. He again positions himself as an expert, and uses the first person plural pronoun 'we' to index collective Tunisian identity. This focus on distinction rather than adequation in terms of relationality appears to be evaluated negatively by Thamena who challenges Alef (Table 8.8, Turn 290).

When he is challenged by Thamena (Turn 290) who asks him what is wrong with being considered Middle Eastern, he again indexes the collective Tunisian identity as he uses the plural pronoun "we feel that er like we are not really represented through the er such labels as the middle East or the Arab world". As the participants move from their initial discourse identities of participant respondents to participant initiators and take more control of the power dynamics of the session, the transportable identities they orient to also shift and become more situated and individualised, thereby denaturalising assumptions of homogeneity within the broad labels used by the Soliya Connect Program.

Table 8.8. Session 1, Turn 282-290

Turn	Speaker	Audio	Text chat
282	Jessica	and what about how erm: are countries like Tunisia Jordan represented IN the United States	
283	silence		
284	Jessica	I mean are they represented as (..) a block? what labels are used the Middle East? North Africa?	
285	silence	(6s)	
286	Jack	or I typically ((cough)) I typically hear Middle East er like in classes and stuff and such we normally use Middle East sometimes (..) North Africa I think (definitely) Middle East (.) is (.) what we: use (.) but °yeah°	Jessica: What lavels are used in US Jessica: to talk about countries like Tunisia, Egypt ...

287	silence	(29s)	Jessica: Jack normally hears Middle East, in class
			Denise: same i normally hear Middle East
			Jessica: and what countries does that include?
288	Alef	(...) because we feel that we are different not the same thing as er not the same people as in Saudi Arabia or in Qatar or in any other country in er the Middle East because we feel that er I dunno maybe North African or Maghrebian would be the appropriate erm er label that we can go under but er er the the (thing) that we share in common same features just like Saudi Arabia or er any other country like (been) we are Arabic Arab at the end and we are Muslim er the same as er: countries of the Middle East but (..) we we consider ourselves not to be Middle Easterns but North African (fully) and erm Maghrebian ( )	Jessica: Alef may Tunisians would not accept the label Middle East
			Jessica: as we feel we are not the same people as eg. in Saudi Arabia, or qatar
			Jessica: maybe north african or Maghrebian would be the mor appropriate label
			Jessica: that we would go under
289	silence	(6s)	Jessica: We are Arab and Muslim like many people in the ME
290	Thamena	Alef just I want to know what what what did you mean by (2s) er you are descent from the people in er USA in Saudi Arabia (I mean) (4s) what's the problem in being from the Middle East	Jessica: but we are also North africans and Maghrebians

8.4. "Because I'm Palestinian"

Another occasion on which participants orient to their transportable identities follows a word associations activity in Session 3 (Table 8.9) where some of the participants are asked why they wrote the words terrorism and criminal in association with Israel. There was considerable negotiation before any of the participants replied, with several requests from participants and facilitators for an explanation before Fadela takes the floor and responds, explicitly indexing her Palestinian identity.

Table 8.9. Session 3, Turn 172-180

Turn	Speaker	Audio	Text chat
172	Fadela	for me I chose the (.) word criminals because I'm Palestinian (I'm erm) (..) I live (..) in Palestine and er in everyday life we see how those people are criminals (..) and I (..) heh (..) can prove to you that they are criminals (...) it's the simple it's the simplest word to describe them	Ranà: as palstinia Jessica: Fadela: I chose the word criminals
173	silence	(3s)	
174	Brendan	what actions rather than um (...) feelings would dictate (...) you:r (.) interpretation er of Israelis as criminals (...) like what, what erm (...) what actions have they committed rather than like (..) everyday things (.) I dunno like yeah I guess like everyday proof (...)	Jessica: because I'm Palestinian and in our every day life Jessica: we experience this Ranà: everyday they proof that they are criminals
175	silence	(3s)	
176	Brendan	I'm I'm not disagreeing I was jus' I'm just curious	
177	silence	(14s)	Jessica: Brendan: What actions have they committed ?What kind of proof?
178	Jessica	yeah in fact er Brendan I think said before that (..) you know that it's it probably comes from our experience of the words that we say the associations we have with words erm and so Fadela your from your experience and others of you are Palestinian too right? can you give us some concrete examples? of your daily life how it affects your daily life ? to help understand	
179	Silence	(9s)	

| 180 | Fadela | erm I want to tell an example of that happened to me in my life, er we have err our house three times er deconstructed by the Israeli by the Israeli soldiers and er we have a lot of prisoners inside the Israeli jails and they suffer a lot they are a lot of a lot of them they have been there for more than thirty years, they have no families no friends nothing to do and erm from the roads between cities | Jessica: Fadela: an example that happened to me |
| | | | Jessica: Our house has 3 times been |

The fact that Fadela was being cast into the discourse identity of 'respondent', repeatedly called upon to explain what was seen as a 'dispreferred response' indicates asymmetry in the power relations at that moment, with Fadela in the 'weaker' position. As if to *authenticate* her response to the word association, Fadela explicitly indexes her Palestinian identity and specifies not only that she is Palestinian but also that she lives in Palestine. She then switches from the first person singular pronoun 'I' to the plural 'we' as she orients to the collective experience of Palestinians living in Palestine, saying she could provide what Stokoe (2012) would define as a 'categorical account' of how "in everyday life *we* see how those people are criminals" (Turn 172). She adds that she "can *prove* to you that they are criminals", which indexes her orientation to the implied assumption that her claims about Israeli identity, and also her own identity are being delegitimised.

Brendan orients to Fadela's offer to provide evidence that can 'prove' the truth claims of her response as he asks her "what actions rather than feelings" dictate her interpretation. Brendan repeats Fadela's reference to the everyday, as he asks her to give examples of Israeli actions which led her to define them as criminals: "what actions have they committed rather than like (..) everyday things (.) I dunno like yeah I guess like everyday proof". There are hesitations and false starts in Brendan's turn and the disclaimer with which he follows up "I'm I'm not disagreeing I was jus' I'm just curious" (Turn 176). This specification can be seen as an attempt to position himself as an intercultural speaker rather than as an adversary who is challenging what Fadela has said.

This exchange also demonstrates how the concept of what Israel means is being negotiated. Brendon's understanding of Israel has inevitably been shaped by the "relational and socio-cultural phenomenon that emerges and circulates in local discourse contexts" (Bucholtz & Hall, 2005, p. 586). In this case, the local discourse context might be US media, politics, and/or discussions with family or friends, and he is being confronted with conflicting views of these concepts. He now needs to reconcile and negotiate new understandings of 'Israel' through interactions with others in situated contexts, facilitated and constrained by power relations (Block, 2007/2014; Norton, 2000/2013; Norton Peirce, 1995).

Fadela responds to Brendan's request after further encouragement from Jessica who reiterates Brendan's previous words regarding experience influencing the associations people make. Jessica's use of the first person plural pronouns "*our* experience" then "the words that *we* say the associations *we* have" emphasises that all people make associations on the basis of their experience, and she is thus authenticating Fadela's response. Her use of first person plural also indexes the group self awareness. Fadela gives an example of what happened to her in her daily life and cites her house being 'deconstructed' by Israeli soldiers three times. She also mentions Palestinians being held in Israeli prisons and the road situation (Turn 180). She thus again explicitly indexes her Palestinian identity and reinforces the identity with which she introduced herself to the group in her blog posts (Chapter 6). Jessica checks her understanding in the next turn (182) as she says she missed what Fadela had said about her house, and Fadela orients to the text mode to repeat what she had originally said, deconstructed – intending demolished or pulled down (making reference to the 'demolition' of Palestinian homes by Israeli soldiers[1]). Jessica does not index the 'non-standard' usage of the word 'deconstruct' but rather 'lets it pass' without requesting further clarification because the meaning of 'deconstructing homes' can be quite easily inferred, though it may not be standard collocation or usage. However, her not following up what Fadela means is a 'missed' opportunity for Brendan's further understanding of the situation in Palestine. The meaning of Fadela's words on a micro level index larger meanings and histories (chronotopes of Israeli

---

1. http://blog.eappi.org/2015/01/

occupation of Palestine) but they may not be sufficient for those who are not familiar with the history of Palestine to understand. Fadela's description of the situation of prisoners is quite clear, but what she meant by the deconstruction of homes, and what she indexes by saying "the roads between the cities" is not. She is clearly making reference to the segregation of roads in Palestine and the fact that Palestinians cannot use Israeli roads and that much of the movement of Palestinians is controlled by the Israeli forces, but the participants may not all be aware of this and her explanation is incomplete.

Doja and Thamena subsequently align to the discourse identity of respondents, following Rana and Brendan's calls for participation. They position themselves as Arab, Jordanian, Palestinian exiles, and this authorises their contributions and authenticates their responses for they are experts of their own lives and their feelings. They build on one another's responses and make reference to family members who were forced to leave Palestine and move to Jordan, the living conditions of relatives in Palestine who they cannot visit, and also make reference to the then recent Cast Lead operation by the Israeli army in Gaza and the deaths of civilians, particularly women and children. It is interesting that neither Thamena nor Doja had indexed their Palestinian identity prior to this session or in their blogs (see Chapter 6). This is thus a discourse identity that is co-constructed in situ between the members and within the group, in alignment with the aim of sharing understanding of others' perspectives. Their responses expand upon and authenticate and authorise Fadela's and their own responses to the word associations activity as they co-construct what living in Palestine means, from the perspective of those who live there or have been exiled, both of which are positions of those who have been and continue to be oppressed.

8.5. "Er I'm bringing up really (..) harsh things erm nine eleven"

The responses of Fadela, Thamena, and Doja in the previous section were challenged by Brendan in a follow-up move (Table 8.10, Turn 203). Brendan's turn can be seen as indicative of resistance to a change in his way of thinking, which is a natural process in 'social-emancipatory view' of 'transformative learning' (a learning theory rooted primarily in the work of Freire, 1984) that is principally based on providing the learner with opportunities for an ontological shift. Such opportunities come about when the learner becomes aware of their own subjectivity (as mentioned in the methodological framework). However, these shifts are often met with initial resistance, as they require the act of critically "questioning our presuppositions underlying our knowledge" (Kreber, 2004, p. 31).

Brendan initiates by acknowledging and expressing understanding of their feelings, and this mitigates the question that follows regarding the legitimacy of their categorisation of Israel as 'criminal' or 'terrorist' in their responses to the trigger words activity and in the discussion that ensued. In his extended turn, Brendan carefully constructs his challenge to their categorisation, which he seeks to do by drawing an analogy with 9/11 in the US. His argument is that he did not use this event (which he categorises as "really harsh things") as a motivation to categorise all Arabs or Afghanis or Iraqis as terrorists, because he recognises that these were the actions of a select few. The implicature is clearly that Palestinians categorising Israel as 'criminal' or 'terrorist' is equivalent to Americans categorising all Arabs or Afghani or Iraqis as terrorists after 9/11, although it was, he says the action of a select few.

Brendan adds a disclaimer, however, saying he "doesn't know enough" to be able to think that there are "hundreds and thousands of Israelis like running through the streets terrorising Palestinians on a daily basis", before reiterating his denaturalisation of the equation israeli=criminal. Deni indexes alignment with Brendan through the text chat, writing that one of her good friends lives in Israel and she would not call him a terrorist or criminal. Her choice of text mode is perhaps less face-threatening for her than the audio-video mode.

Thamena takes the floor to respond to Brendan, challenging his analogy and saying that the situation is different. It is through indexing of her Palestinian identity that she authenticates her words as she describes the impact of Israel's actions on her life being that she cannot enter "her land". Thamena seems to have found agency through her Palestinian identity which she has disclosed and through the co-construction with the group of an understanding of life in Palestine and the impact of Israeli occupation on their daily lives.

Mohammed too challenges Brendan through the aural mode with an extended turn, and Fadela engages with both Brendan and Deni through the text chat to challenge what they have said and further express her point of view. The multiple threads (which are too long to include in their entirety) and intensity of the exchange index the participants' investment in this topic of interaction and the desire to transmit and explain feelings and experiences.

Table 8.10. Session 3, Turns 203-205

Turn	Speaker	Audio	Text chat
203	Brendan	uhm (1s) I understand (..) the intense feelings that ( ) that into account but erm do you think that there is enough (..) of the population like particiaping in these er criminal acts to group an enti:re country of I'm not exactly sure the Israeli population into one word as extremist terrorist or criminals 'hh because I mean um what nine eleven I'm not er I'm bringing up really (..) harsh things erm nine eleven uh I still don't think like erm when someone says Arab or Afghani or Iraqi my first thought isn't criminal or: terrorist (.) it was just a select few of people I don't know enough to like think that there are like erm hundreds of thousands of Israelis like running through the streets terrorising Palestinians on a daily basis but i just don't think it's ( ) generalise enough erm (amount) of the population to see such harsh accusations fo:r an entire country to be summed up in one a word like that	Jessica: Mohammed: what else can we say about these massacres Jessica: Brendan: I understand the intense feelings but do you think that there are enough persons Jessica: involved to classify the whole of Israel as criminals Jessica: Brendan: eg. after 9/11 my first thought when Arab is mentioned I don't immediately think of terrorist

204	silence	(8s)		Denise: one of my good friends lives in Israel right now and I would not call him a terrorist or a criminal
205	Thamena	I think the situation for us is different because I'm a Palestinian and they took my land they live there and they prevent me to to enter my land then even the Israelis civils or nationals who don't er fight or don't participate in the wars they support the soldiers and support the government of Israel		Jessica: Brendan: I don't know if I see enough of a generalised action across the whole country to accuse
				Jessica: all Israelis

A little later on in the session (Table 8.11, Turn 258), Fadela returns to the issue of Palestine and Israel and orients to Brendan as she asks him a question. She does not release the floor to give Brendan the opportunity to answer, but continues with an extended turn where once again she positions herself as Palestinian and describes the "day of the land" which was being celebrated that day. She explains why this is celebrated and addresses Brendan as she says midway in her turn "I want to remind you of an important point" and indexes the history of Israel and the Balfour declaration[2]. She is providing further 'proof' to authenticate her categorisation of Israel which Brendan had challenged, and she frames the conflict as a war, which is a result of historical events and Western intervention. She acknowledges the images in the media and common stereotypes as regards Palestinians, but she calls on critical judgement of people to distinguish between 'the right and the wrong'. Again, it appears that the Palestinian identity gives her both the authority and the 'passion of experience'. As Kramsch (2013) writes, "as the subject comes into being in interaction with others, desire – as positive or negative identification with the other – is by essence dialogic and intersubjective" (p. 35).

---

2. On November 2nd 1917, British Foreign Secretary Lord Arthur James Balfour made a promise (now known as the Balfour Declaration) to the Zionist movement that the British government favoured the establishment of a Jewish homeland in Palestine (For text see http://www.history.com/this-day-in-history/the-balfour-declaration). Jack Straw told New Statesman in 2002: "A lot of the problems we are having to deal with now, are a consequence of our colonial past…The Balfour declaration and the contradictory assurances which were being given to Palestinians in private at the same time as they were being given to the Israelis – again, an interesting history for us but not an entirely honourable one" (https://www. newstatesman.com/node/156641)

In the end, all three of the main participants in this exchange (Brendon, Thamena, and Fadela) seem to recognise their own intersubjectivities of individuals who are shaped by the socio-political discourse around them but acknowledge, and appropriate, the possibility of agentivity to change and to change others. As explained in the theoretical framework, subjectivity makes reference to the way the subject positions herself and/or is positioned through discourse and is socially and historically embedded. It is thus dynamic, contradictory, and changes over time and space, which we can witness occurring here in this session.

Table 8.11. Session 3, Turn 258

Turn	Speaker	Audio	Text chat
258	Fadela	(3s) I just want to ask Brendan a question (1s) and I'm waiting an ( ) answer (1s) do you have tv at home? and that's (only) the question today as Palestinians we celebrate the day of the land 'hh and tradition we do (2s) we do (2s) erm we do plant trees olive trees er which is totally symbolic 'hh for our resistance our (concentration) to er to: make our lands free from Israel 'hh and to live peacefully here in our (land) Palestine (1s) and this year there is something new I want to share with you there will be er: a plant (1s) for every (person) ever prisoner the Israelis killed and for every martyr (1s) who they killed during the (2s) the war between us and Israel 'hh and I want to to remind you of an important point 'hh that because of the presence of Israel (3s) was in er 1914 I think it was Balfour promised to give erm to give the Jews the land (1s) but he he didn't own the land its our land and they give this land to (1s) those people who call them (Zion) states (..) so we have to remin remember all these events (1s) and we have we all have tv at home and we can see the news I know that there is a wrong image in the media (1s) or a stereotypical image about er the Palestinian Iraeli situation (1s) but I think that er every everyone has (1s) er has his own brain and he can think and er and the difference (the brain) the right and the wrong thank you hh	Ranà: do u think that voices u r hearing now reperesents what is presented on the media? Ranà: regarding the palastinian suffering everyday Jessica: Fadela: today as Palestinians we celebrate the day of the land Jessica: we plant olive trees Jessica: this year there will be a plant for every martyr who has been killed in the war between us and Israel Jessica: we have to remember all the events, the history Jessica: I know there is a wrong image in the media

8.6. Prospective and imagined identities

As I discussed in Chapter 5, the situated context of the Soliya Connect Program also offers a 'prospective identity' in which the participants are invited to 'invest', which links to Norton's (2000/2013) notion of 'imagined identity'. What emerged from the analysis of the website and Soliya Connect Program materials is a strong prospective identity for participants as a new generation of "influencers" who can "alleviate tensions when they emerge and collaboratively address the challenges of the 21st Century"[3]. The members of this community can be likened to "networked cosmopolitans" (Williamson, 2013, p. 46) who share the beliefs and goals of the Soliya Connect Program; they engage with difference and can 'shift from dialogue to action'. Opportunities to fulfil this prospect are offered through further engagement with Soliya, for example facilitation training, becoming a volunteer facilitator, coach, and even trainer[4].

The extent to which this imagined prospective identity emerged in the interactions varied. The dialogue in the last part of the final session was intended to bring these imagined and prospective identities to the fore as the facilitators asked the participants about how they saw the future and their role in fostering change. On an individual level, some members suggested engaging with difference through reading about other cultures, participating in projects like Model United Nations or talking to members of their community about their experience in Soliya and seeking to foster other similar experiences[5]. The sense of agency of the group as a whole was expressed in terms of creating a group or becoming friends on Facebook so they could remain in touch with one another, which some of them did. However, analysis of the interaction alone cannot provide information about further engagement. What is required is a long-term study of participants – which was not among the original aims of this study.

---

3. The original text and webpage can no longer be found.

4. On the website, Soliya report that research carried out in collaboration with MIT has found that 30% of the Soliya Connect Program alumni go on to take the facilitation training after completion of the program as an indication of their "desire to continue to be engaged and to take a leadership role in fostering international understanding"; https://www.soliya.net/programs/connect-program

5. MIT's findings indicate that 90% shared information about what they were learning with their peers and other people in their community; https://www.soliya.net/programs/connect-program

I did, however, succeed in contacting two of the participants, Mohammed and Alef, five years after their participation in the Soliya Connect Program, and I carried out interviews over email and Skype to acquire further information in this respect. Mohammed, who has become an English teacher, reported that he was no longer in contact with the members of the dialogue group, they had not had enough time perhaps to create a strong bond. Nonetheless, he writes that he has a robust and positive memory of the experience and the feeling of belonging to a group, and he also refers to the impact the Soliya Connect Program had on him and the way he relates to difference:

> "Well, I think the period was not long enough for us to get to know each other to that extent or to merge but, I know for sure if we had had longer time, we would have done since I until this moment still remember these days because I considered myself part of that group. [...] I am not in touch with my group because of the busy life and so on but I have met coincidentally other Soliya members and facilitators and we keep in touch from time to another. Well now I am aware of the meaning of difference not conflict. I have to listen before judge and of course now I am a flexible person as I accept the others no matter how they think or believe in. It's personal perspectives and we should respect it" (Mohammed, personal communication, 2016).

Alef's identity had emerged through the interaction as a student leader, a young person who was active in his local context organising volunteers to support refugees on the border with Libya, interested in the political situation of his region and strongly invested in the Soliya Connect Program. His active – and at times dominant participation in the online sessions reflected in many ways his offline identities. He continued to engage with Soliya through facilitator training and facilitation and participation in a regional workshop in Jordan. He reported that participation in the Soliya Connect Program had opened up his experience of the world (which until then had been limited to the Tunisian context) to a more international outlook and network of contacts. He became friends with many members of the Soliya network and has met some of them face to face after years of being friends online. He had written on his blog that in ten years' time he saw himself as being an English teacher somewhere in the Arab world. In a Skype interview he told me that he did graduate in English language and literature, however partly due to his experience of Soliya he had become interested in the media and indeed obtained a job with the BBC Media Action in Tunisia. He believes that his experience with Soliya was key to his obtaining this position for he discussed it extensively in his interview as it was the first international experience he had had. As we discussed the notion of 'imagined identities', he was able to identify with this, and found the concept of the 'networked cosmopolitan' to reflect how he saw himself.

Alef was exceptional in the dialogue group. He was the only one who participated not as a part of his university studies, but on an individual basis, because he had heard about it through a friend and wanted to participate as he was very drawn to it. He was already interculturally curious and aware, and had the digital literacies to be able to use the multimodal tools from the very first session in order to make his voice heard and even set the topic for discussion. Though he attributes great importance to Soliya in his career trajectory, it is likely that he would have found other opportunities. As regards the other group members, I have not been able to contact them to explore this issue.

8.7. Discussion

What I have sought to do in this chapter is take some excerpts from the interactions that took place in this situated context of virtual exchange to explore how participants orient to transportable identities and how this can influence power dynamics in the interactions. What was relevant and empowering about the identities that the participants indexed was not the categories in themselves, but rather how indexing them allowed the participants to re-position themselves in the interactions, as 'experts of their own experiences'. It was bringing their experiences to a group whose shared interest was acquiring greater understanding about 'recent events' in Egypt and Tunisia, or the relationship between Palestine and Israel, Middle East and US, that changed the dynamics. This allowed students who, for example, positioned themselves as language learners or who may have been cast by others into a subordinate position due to the fact that they were facing technical difficulties due to poor Internet connections, or because their responses to questions were being challenged, or because they live in a part of the world which is considered 'developing' and in need of 'help', to reposition themselves and challenge dominant discourses.

Bringing their experience, different ways of knowing to a group where some members did not have much knowledge or access to people in their regions created the condition for many of the participants to 'claim a voice', although some had to do so in a foreign language, and for many this new online environment presented initial challenges. It was when they were talking about topics which they were familiar with, curious to learn more about, or felt strongly about that they *invested* more in the interactions, taking extended turns and working to make themselves 'heard' and 'understood'.

bell hooks (1994) uses the phrase "passion of experience" to describe these ways of knowing through experience, which encompass many feelings, above all suffering, "for there is a particular knowledge that comes from suffering. It is a way of knowing that is often expressed through the body, what it knows, what has been deeply inscribed on it through experience. This complexity of experience can rarely be voiced and named from a distance" (p. 91).

The 'special' knowledge that can be acquired through listening to experiences, confessions, and testimonies is a vital dimension of the learning process in critical pedagogies, allowing individuals to engage with different standpoints and to gain a fuller and more inclusive understanding than engaging only with analytical ways of knowing. Experiential knowledge can enhance our learning experience, it is a way of knowing that can coexist in a nonhierarchical way with other ways of knowing. At the same time, shifting paradigms can make participants feel discomfort and even pain for, as hooks (1994) writes, "it may hurt them that new ways of knowing may create estrangement where there was none" (p. 43).

CHAPTER 9

Final considerations

This book is based on an understanding of identity as being discursively constructed and reconstituted every time we engage in interaction. This implies that just as contexts and practices can limit opportunities for learners to engage in identity work, contexts and practices can also be designed to offer learners enhanced possibilities for social interaction and positioning. This is one of the aims of virtual exchange as conceptualised in this book. So what kind of virtual exchange contexts can and should we design to offer enhanced possibilities for these kinds of interaction? Here I have explored one particular model of virtual exchange, but of course there is no one solution that 'fits all'. What I seek to do here in this final chapter is not provide guidelines, but consider some of the implications of this study and ask questions that as educators we can reflect on as we design and integrate virtual exchange into our activity. I then close with recent developments as regards virtual exchange on the policy level, and the implications this has for educators working in the field.

In relation to the situatedness principle of the framework presented in this book and its application to our own contexts we might ask ourselves what are the identity positionings that we make relevant for our students? What kind of structural and power asymmetries are embedded in these contexts and identities and how can we address them?

Educational contexts are never neutral, hence the importance of exploring and reflecting upon the assumptions underlying our practice. Furthermore, all contexts of interaction have power dimensions embedded within them. What we can learn from the fields of conflict transformation and peace studies (Agbaria & Cohen, 2000; Saunders, 1999) which have fed into the design of the virtual exchange explored in this study is the importance of being aware of structural power asymmetries, observing and reflecting on interaction and power dynamics, and having tools and strategies to challenge them. Nonetheless, becoming aware of and seeking to address asymmetries in power does not mean that they will disappear (Bali, 2014).

The concepts of 'imagined identities' and student investment in learning can be useful tools in reflecting on the situated virtual exchange contexts we develop. In this study, the imagined identity proposed by Soliya was likened to the 'networked cosmopolitan', an individual with a particular interest in engaging with the 'other' through their transnational network and working towards a more empathetic society. As regards the virtual exchange contexts we create for our students we might ask what prospective identities does it make relevant? Are these of interest to the students? How do these relate to the social world and current issues around us?

Teacher education is one area in which virtual exchange is increasingly being adopted with the aim of preparing future teachers with the experience and desire to design and implement virtual exchanges once they have their own classes (Dooly & Sadler, 2013, 2016; Dooly & O'Dowd, 2018). In virtual exchanges which involve pre-service teachers and students of education, there is a clear prospective identity that participants share – the networked teacher with intercultural awareness and digital literacies, members of a transnational community of practice (Dooly, 2013, 2015a, 2015b; Dooly & Tudini, 2016; Sànchez & Manrique, 2018).

In relation to the mediation principle, we might want to ask ourselves to what extent are we aware of the affordances of the tools we are using for interaction? Do we give students the opportunity to develop awareness of how multiple modes can be used effectively (Guichon & Cohen, 2016) for interaction and identity construction?

As Thorne, Sauro, and Smith (2015) write: "enhancing one's ability to be agile and adept across communicative modalities should be a primary focus of instructed L2 education" (p. 229). Offering students opportunities for interaction in a range of modalities and for understanding and exploring the affordances of different tools for different purposes is one way of doing this. This entails teachers developing semio-pedagogical competence (Develotte, Guichon, & Vincent, 2010) and being able to assess the affordances of each medium for identity work. Kern (2015) suggests that we should foster learners' reflection on how people create social identities in the process of designing meaning in speech, writing, and gesture. One way of doing this would be to engage them in a similar analysis to what I have done in this thesis, have them observe video recordings of their interactions. Kern and colleagues have called it 'la salle de retrospection' (Kern, 2014), whereby their student partners would watch, review, and reflect on recordings of their interactions, a practice also undertaken with teacher trainees (Guichon & Cohen, 2016).

Finally, in relation to the principles of positionality, indexicality, and relationality, we might ask ourselves whether we create opportunities for our students to have a wider range of discourse identities? How can we involve students in interactions where they engage not only in adequation to others, but also distinction, where they can disagree and challenge one another and ask questions which seek to acquire greater understanding of an issue? In what ways can we bring students' transportable identities into play? To what extent can we challenge and denaturalise essentialist and commonsense assumptions as regards identities? How can we raise students' awareness of the ways in which identities can and indeed are used (implicitly and explicitly) to position people and empower or disempower them?

In order for students feel comfortable disagreeing with and challenging one another it is important to create a safe space in which this can happen. Before engaging in deep discussions, students generally need to break the ice and get to know one another, and they also need to communicate on a sustained basis to reach a level of trust where they may be able to express what they feel. In the model of virtual exchange explored in this study, it was facilitators that supported participants in creating this kind of space, leading them through the group process so they established a collective identity that could be likened to a community of inquiry (Hauck, Galley, & Warnecke, 2016). While the facilitators maintained an institutional identity through most of the interactions, the participants engaged in a range of identity positionings and also discourse identities – advancing beliefs, challenging one another, and explaining and evaluating arguments. Through collective reflections on the interactions the participants re-aligned to one another and the group at the end of each session. Clearly all groups, and indeed facilitators, are different, as are their interactions, and the findings of this study cannot be generalised to other groups or educational contexts. Facilitators in this case were not teachers or content experts, but rather facilitators of a process. The extent to which orientation to this kind of facilitator identity is desirable or indeed feasible for teachers will clearly vary on individual and situational factors.

Since I embarked on the original study which formed the basis of this book many things have changed. On the geo-political level, since the interactions took place the so-called 'Arab Springs' in Tunisia and Egypt have not brought about the change that was hoped for[1]. Syria, which was the last country to engage in a people-led revolution, is now devastated by a war which has led to the deaths of hundreds of thousands and the displacement of millions of people. Palestinians continue to live, and protest, under occupation with over a hundred casualties in this year alone. At the time of writing the European Council[2] has decided to strengthen borders and close the Mediterranean route into Europe – which will inevitably lead to further deaths in the Mediterranean, the 'graveyard of European values'[3]. In the United States migrant children and families face indefinite detention and separation if caught crossing the US border illegally[4]. Populist right-wing parties are gaining popularity and winning elections in Europe[5] and beyond, xenophobic populism and hate speech are, unsurprisingly, on the rise[6].

---

1. https://www.theguardian.com/books/2016/jan/23/arab-spring-five-years-on-writers-look-back

2. https://reliefweb.int/report/world/european-council-conclusions-28-june-2018

3. https://www.aljazeera.com/indepth/opinion/2015/04/mediterranean-graveyard-european-values-150422050428476.html

4. https://www.theguardian.com/us-news/2018/jun/30/migrant-children-and-families-now-face-indefinite-detention-by-us

5. https://foreignpolicy.com/2018/05/21/in-europe-the-only-choice-is-right-or-far-right/

6. https://www.coe.int/t/dghl/monitoring/ecri/activities/Annual_Reports/Annual%20report%202017.pdf

The need to make stronger links between conflict transformation, peace studies and intercultural dialogue seem to be coming closer as our societies face times of increased tensions and hate towards the 'other'. Policy makers (in some spheres) are calling on educators and educational institutions to address these tensions.

In terms of virtual exchange there have been important developments on a policy level with substantial investments. In the US, the Chris Stevens Initiative "a public-private initiative"[7] was launched in 2015 and is seeking to promote collaborative projects between the US, Middle East, and North Africa. The European Commission launched the Erasmus+ Virtual Exchange project at the beginning of 2018, which targets Europe and the Southern Mediterranean and aims to "promote intercultural dialogue and improve the skills of at least 25,000 young people through digital learning tools over the next two years"[8]. This latter initiative brings together the two approaches to virtual exchange described in Chapter one, telecollaboration, which regards small-scale projects developed bottom-up by partner teachers, and the type of online facilitated dialogue explored in this study. Online facilitated dialogue, such as the Soliya Connect Program, is one of the activities that this pilot project is promoting. Another activity is training for educators to collaboratively design curricula for transdisciplinary virtual exchange projects that are supported with synchronous facilitated dialogues[9].

This increased interest for virtual exchange is no doubt good news, but at the same time it raises some concerns. Like other educational activities that receive funding, virtual exchange is a form of 'soft power'[10]. There is a risk that it can be 'hijacked' to meet neo-liberal interests, governments' political and ideological agendas, and be used as a tool not to foster greater understanding and mutual

---

7. http://stevensinitiative.org

8. http://europa.eu/rapid/press-release_IP-18-1741_en.htm

9. https://europa.eu/youth/erasmusvirtual_en

10. https://ec.europa.eu/education/sites/education/files/erasmus-virtual-exchange-study_en.pdf

engagement with different perspectives and complexity, but rather to further exacerbate inequalities. As Bali (2014) writes,

> "[d]ialogue can be potentially colonizing, as it empowers one group by inherently being on their terms and serving their interests (Burbules, 2000; Gorski, 2008; Jones, 1999). Even benign dialogue can provide colonizers with a tool for 'surveillance and exploitation' (Bhabha, 1994, p. 99, cited in Jones, 1999, p. 309)" (pp. 213-214).

Virtual exchange has the potential to challenge the hegemonising forces of neoliberal, colonial approaches to foreign language teaching (Train, 2010), international education, and applications of education technologies. It is important however that we, as educators, practitioners, and/or researchers, constantly assess and interrogate policies, practices, and perspectives.

References

Agbaria, F., & Cohen, C. (2000). *Working with groups in conflict: the impact of power relations on the dynamics of the group*. Informally published article, Brandeis University. http://www.brandeis.edu/ethics/pdfs/publications/Working_Groups.pdf

Ahearn, L. (2001). Language and agency. *Annual Review of Anthropology, 30*, 109-137. https://doi.org/10.1146/annurev.anthro.30.1.109

Anderson, B. (1991). *Imagined communities: reflections on the origin and spread of nationalism* (Revised edition). Verso.

Andreotti, V. (2005). *Briefing. Open spaces for dialogue and enquiry methodology*. http://www.osdemethodology.org.uk/keydocs/osdebriefing.pdf

Andreotti, V., & de Souza, L. M. (2008). Global learning in the 'knowledge society'; four tools for discussion. *ZEP, 31*(1), 9-14.

Androutsopoulos, J. (2008). Potentials and limitations of discourse-centred online ethnography. *Language@Internet, 5*. http://www.languageatinternet.org/articles/2008/1610

Androutsopoulos, J. (2013). Code-switching in computer-mediated communication. In S. S. Herring, D. Stein & T. Virtanen (Eds), *Pragmatics of computer-mediated communication*. De Gruyter Mouton. https://doi.org/10.1515/9783110214468.667

Androutsopoulos, J., & Juffermans, K. (2014). Digital language practices in superdiversity: introduction. *Discourse, Context and Media, 4-5*, 1-6. https://doi.org/10.1016/j.dcm.2014.08.002

Antaki, C., & Widdicombe, S. (Eds). (1998). *Identities in talk*. Sage.

Appadurai, A. (1996). *Modernity at large: cultural dimensions of globalization*. University of Minnesota Press.

Argo, N., Idriss, S., & Fancy, M. (2009). *Media and intergroup relations: research on media and social change*. https://www.scribd.com/document/91030506/Media-and-Intergroup-Relations-Research-on-Media-and-Social-Change

Bakhtin, M. (1986). *Speech genres and other late essays*. University of Texas Press.

Bali, M. (2013). *Critical thinking in context: practice at an american liberal arts university in Egypt*. Unpublished PhD dissertation. University of Sheffield, UK. http://dar.aucegypt.edu/handle/10526/3721

References

Bali, M. (2014). Why doesn't this feel empowering? The challenges of web-based intercultural dialogue. *Teaching in Higher Education, 19*(2), 208-215. https://doi.org/10.1080/135625 17.2014.867620

Bali, M., & Bossone, A. (2010). *Intercultural and multicultural education in universities and studies: a comparison of two programs implemented at the American University in Cairo.* The Arab-Turkish Congress of Social Sciences, Ankara.

Bali, M., & Sharma, S. (2014). Bonds of difference: participation as inclusion. *Hybrid Pedagogy.* http://www.digitalpedagogylab.com/hybridped/bonds-difference-participation-inclusion/

Barbot, M.-J., & Dervin, F. (Eds). (2011). *Rencontres interculturelles et formation.* Éducation Permanente.

Belz, J. A. (2002). Social dimensions of telecollaborative foreign language study. *Language Learning & Technology, 6*(1), 60-81.

Belz, J. A. (2003). Linguistic perspectives on the development of intercultural competence in telecollaboration. *Language Learning & Technology, 7*(2), 68-99. https://doi. org/10125/25201

Belz, J. A. (2007). The development of intercultural communicative competence in telecollaborative partnerships. In R. O'Dowd (Ed.), *Online intercultural exchange: an introduction for foreign language teachers* (pp. 127-166). Multilingual Matters.

Belz, J. A., & Kinginger, C. (2003). Discourse options and the development of pragmatic competence by classroom learners of German: the case of address forms. *Language Learning, 53*, 591-647. https://doi.org/10.1046/j.1467-9922.2003.00238.x

Belz, J. A., & Thorne, S. L. (Eds). (2006). *Internet-mediated intercultural foreign language education.* Thomson Heinle.

Bemporad, C., & Jeanneret, T. (2016). L'investissement dans la littératie : identités sociales et capital symbolique. *Langage et société, 157*, 39-45. https://doi.org/10.3917/ls.157.0039

Bezemer, J., & Jewitt, C. (2010). Multimodal analysis. In L. Litosseliti (Ed.), *Research methods in linguistics* (pp. 180-197). Continuum.

Bhabha, H. (1994). *The location of culture.* Routledge.

Black, R. W. (2009). Online fan fiction, global identities, and imagination. *Research in the Teaching of English, 43*, 397-425.

Blake, R. (2000). Computer mediated communication: a window on L2 Spanish interlanguage. *Language Learning & Technology, 4*(1), 120-136.

Block, D. (2007/2014). *Second language identities.* Continuum/Bloomsbury.

Blommaert, J. (1991). How much culture is there in intercultural communication? In J. Blommaert & J. Verschueren (Eds), *The pragmatics of intercultural and international communication*. John Benjamins. https://doi.org/10.1075/pbns.6.3.03blo

Blommaert, J. (2015). Chronotopic identities. *Tilburg Papers in Culture Studies, 144*. https://www.academia.edu/t/a-KkeEUPs-Pv7H1/15207208/Chronotopic_identities

Blommaert, J., & de Fina, A. (2015). Chronotopic identities: on the timespace organization of who we are. *Tilburg Papers in Culture Studies, 153*. https://www.researchgate.net/publication/287331436_Chronotopic_Identitiesr

Boden, D., & Zimmerman, D. H. (1991). *Talk and social studies in ethnomethodology and conversation analysis*. Polity Press.

Borghetti, C. (2011). How to teach it? Proposal for a methodological model of intercultural competence. In A. Witte & T. Harden (Eds), *Intercultural competence: concepts, challenges, evaluations* (pp. 141-160). Peter Lang.

Bourdieu, P. (1977). The economics of linguistic exchanges. *Social Science Information, 16*(6), 645-668. https://doi.org/10.1177/053901847701600601

Bourdieu, P. (1984). *Distinction: a social critique of the judgment of taste* (Translated by Richard Nice). Routledge & Kegan Paul.

Bourdieu, P. (1990). *The logic of practice*. Stanford University Press.

Bourdieu, P. (1991). *Language and Symbolic Power* (Edited by J. B. Thompson, translated by G. Raymond & M. Adamson). Polity Press. (Original work published in 1982.)

Bourdieu, P., & Passeron, J.-C. (1990). *Reproduction in education, society and culture*. Sage.

boyd, d. (2006). *Identity production in a networked culture: why youth heart MySpace*. American Association for the Advancement of Science.

boyd, d. (2008). Why youth ♥ social network sites: the role of networked publics in teenage social life. In D. Buckingham (Ed.), *Youth, identity, and digital media. The John D. and Catherine T. MacArthur Foundation Series on Digital Media and Learning* (pp. 119-142). The MIT Press.

boyd, d., & Ellison N. B. (2007). Social networks: definition, history, and scholarship. *Journal of Computer-Mediated Communication, 13*(1). https://doi.org/10.1111/j.1083-6101.2007.00393.x

Brown, P., & Levinson, S. C. (1987). *Politeness: some universals in language usage*. Cambridge University Press. https://doi.org/10.1017/CBO9780511813085

References

Bucholtz, M. (1999). "Why Be Normal?": Language and identity practices in a community of nerd girls. *Language in Society, 28*(2), 203-223. https://doi.org/10.1017/ S0047404599002043

Bucholtz, M. (2003). Sociolinguistic nostalgia and the authentication of identity. *Journal of Sociolinguistics, 7*(3), 398-416. https://doi.org/10.1111/1467-9481.00232

Bucholtz, M., & Hall, K. (2004a). Language and identity. In A. Duranti (Ed.), *A companion to linguistic anthropology* (pp. 369-94). Blackwell.

Bucholtz, M., & Hall, K. (2004b). Theorizing identity in language and sexuality research. *Language in Society, 33*(4), 501-47. https://doi.org/10.1017/S0047404504334020

Bucholtz, M., & Hall, K. (2005). Identity and interaction: a socio-cultural linguistic approach. *Discourse Studies, 7*(4-5), 585-614. https://doi.org/10.1177/1461445605054407

Buckingham, D. (Ed.). (2008). *Youth, identity and digital media*. The MIT Press.

Burbules, N. C. (2000). The limits of dialogue as a critical pedagogy. In P. P. Trifonas (Ed.), *Revolutionary pedagogies: cultural politics, instituting education, and the discourse of theory* (pp. 251-273). Routledge.

Burgess, H. (2005). Activism. In G. Burgess & H. Burgess (Eds), *Beyond intractability*. Conflict Information Consortium, University of Colorado, Boulder.

Butler, J. (1990). *Gender trouble: feminism and the subversion of identity*. Routledge.

Byrnes, H. (2004). Perspectives. *The Modern Language Journal, 88*(2), 266-291. https://doi. org/10.1111/j.0026-7902.2004.00229.x

Camicia, S. P., & Franklin, B. (2010). Curriculum reform in a globalized world: the discourse of cosmopolitanism and community. *London Review of Education, 8*(2), 93-104. https:// doi.org/10.1080/14748460.2010.487327

Carroll, L. (2000). *Alice's adventures in Wonderland & through the looking-glas*. Penguin Group.

Charalambous, C. (2014). "Whether you see them as friends or enemies you need to know their language." Turkish language learning in a Greek-Cypriot school. In V. Lytra (Ed.), *When Greeks and Turks meet: interdisciplinary perspectives on the relationship since 1923* (pp. 141-162). Routledge.

Chen, H. I. (2013). Identity practices of multilingual writers in social networking spaces. *Language Learning & Technology, 17*(2), 143-170. http://llt.msu.edu/issues/june2013/chen.pdf

Chun, D. M., & Plass, J. L. (2000). Networked multimedia environments for second language acquisition. In M. Warschauer & R. Kern (Eds), *Network-based language teaching: concepts and practice* (pp. 151-170). Cambridge University Press. https://doi.org/10.1017/ CBO9781139524735.009

Cook, B. J. (1999). Islamic versus Western conceptions of education: reflections on Egypt. *International Review of Education, 45*(3/4), 339-357. https://doi.org/10.1023/A:1003808525407

Cummins, J., & Sayers, D. (1995). *Brave new schools: challenging cultural illiteracies through global learning networks.* St. Martin's Press.

Darvin, R., & Norton, B. (2015). Identity and a model of investment in applied linguistics. *Annual Review of Applied Linguistics, 35,* 36-56. https://doi.org/10.1017/S0267190514000191

Davies, A. (2003). *The native speakers: myth and reality.* Multilingual Matters.

Davies, B., & R. Harré (1990). Positioning: the discursive production of selves. *Journal for the Theory of Social Behaviour, 20*(1), 43-63. https://doi.org/10.1111/j.1468-5914.1990.tb00174.x

Deppermann, A. (2000). Ethnographische Gesprächsanalyse. *Gesprächsforschung, 1,* 96-124. http://www.gespraechsforschung-ozs.de/heft2000/ga-deppermann.pdf

Dervin, F. (2013). International sociodigital interaction: what politics of interculturality? In F. Sharifian & M. Jamarani (Eds), *Language and intercultural communication in the new era* (pp. 83-98). Routledge.

Dervin, F. (2015). Towards post-intercultural teacher education: analysing 'extreme' intercultural dialogue to reconstruct interculturality. *European Journal of Teacher Education, 38*(1), 71-86. https://doi.org/10.1080/02619768.2014.902441

Develotte, C., Guichon, N., & Vincent, C. (2010). The use of the webcam for teaching a foreign language in a desktop videoconferencing environment. *ReCALL, 22,* 293-312. https://doi.org/10.1017/S0958344010000170

Dooly, M. (2008). *Telecollaborative language learning.* Peter Lang.

Dooly, M. (2011). Crossing the intercultural borders into 3rd space culture(s): implications for teacher education in the twenty-first century. *Language and Intercultural Communication, 11*(4), 319-337. https://doi.org/10.1080/14708477.2011.599390

Dooly, M. (2013). Focusing on the social: research into the distributed knowledge of novice teachers in online exchange. In C. Meskill (Ed.), *Online teaching and learning: sociocultural perspectives. Advances in digital language learning and teaching* (pp. 137-155). Bloomsbury Academic.

Dooly, M. (2015a). It takes research to build a community: ongoing challenges for scholars in digitally-supported communicative language teaching. *Calico Journal, 32*(1), 172-194. https://doi.org/10.1558/calico.v32i1.25664

Dooly, M. (2015b). Networked classrooms and networked minds: language teaching in a brave new world. In C. J. Jenks & P. Seedhouse (Eds), *International perspectives on the ELT classroom* (pp. 84-109). Palgrave MacMillan. https://doi.org/10.1057/9781137340733_6

Dooly, M., & Hauck, M. (2012). Researching multimodal communicative competence in video and audio telecollaborative encounters. In M. Dooly & R. O'Dowd (Eds), *Researching online foreign language interaction and exchange: theories, methods and challenges* (pp. 135-161). Peter Lang.

Dooly, M., & O'Dowd, R. (Eds). (2012). *Researching online foreign language interaction and exchange theories, methods and challenges.* Peter Lang. https://doi.org/10.3726/978-3-0351-0414-1

Dooly, M., & O'Dowd, R. (2018). Telecollaboration in the foreign language classroom: a review of its origins and its application to language teaching practice. In M. Dooly & R. O'Dowd (Eds), *In this together: teachers' experiences with transnational, telecollaborative language learning projects* (pp. 11-34). Peter Lang.

Dooly, M., & Sadler, R. (2013). Filling in the gaps: linking theory and practice through telecollaboration in teacher education. *ReCALL, 25*(1), 4-29. https://doi.org/10.1017/S0958344012000237

Dooly, M., & Sadler, R. (2016). Becoming little scientists: technologically-enhanced project-based language learning. Language Learning & Technology, 20(1), 54-78.

Dooly, M., & Tudini, V. (2016). Now we are teachers: the role of small talk in student language teachers' telecollaborative task development. *Journal of Pragmatics, 102,* 38-53. https://doi.org/10.1016/j.pragma.2016.06.008

Dooly, M., & Vallejo Rubinstein, C. (2017). Bridging across languages and cultures in everyday lives: an expanding role for critical intercultural communication. *Language and Intercultural Communication, 18*(1), 1-8. https://doi.org/10.1080/14708477.2017.1400508

Du Bois, J. W. (2007). The stance triangle. In R. Englebretson (Ed.), *Stancetaking in discourse: subjectivity, evaluation, interaction* (pp.139-182). Benjamins.

Duranti, A. (1997). *Linguistic anthropology.* Cambridge University Press. https://doi.org/10.1017/CBO9780511810190

European Commission. (2013). *Report to the European Commission on improving the quality of teaching and learning in Europe's higher education institutions.* Publications office of the European Union. http://ec.europa.eu/dgs/education_culture/repository/education/library/reports/modernisation_en.pdf

Finch, J., & Nynäs, P. (2011). *Transforming otherness.* Transactions.

Firth, A. (1996). The discursive accomplishment of normality: on 'lingua franca' English and conversation analysis. *Journal of Pragmatics, 26*(2), 237-259. https://doi.org/10.1016/0378-2166(96)00014-8

Firth, A. (2009). Doing not being a foreign language learner: English as a lingua franca in the workplace and (some) implications for SLA. *International Review of Applied Linguistics in Language Teaching, 47*(1), 127-156. https://doi.org/10.1515/iral.2009.006

Firth, A., & Wagner, J. (1997). On discourse, communication and (some) fundamental concepts in SLA research. *The Modern Language Journal, 81*(3), 285-300. https://doi.org/10.1111/j.1540-4781.1997.tb05480.x

Freire, P. (1984). *Pedagogy of the oppressed.* Continuum.

Galley, R., Conole, G., & Panagiota, A. (2014). Community indicators: a framework for observing and supporting community activity on Cloudworks. *Interactive Learning Environments, 22*(3), 373-395. https://doi.org/10.1080/10494820.2012.680965

Gardner, R. (2012). Conversation analysis in the classroom. In J. Sidnell & T. Stivers (Eds), *The handbook of conversation analysis* (pp. 593-611). Wiley-Blackwell. https://doi.org/10.1002/9781118325001.ch29

Garfinkel, H. (1967). *Studies in Ethnomethodology.* Polity.

Garrison, D. R., Anderson, T., & Archer, W. (2000). Critical inquiry in a text-based environment: computer conferencing in higher education. *The Internet and Higher Education, 2*(2-3), 87-105. https://doi.org/10.1016/S1096-7516(00)00016-6

Gee, E. H., & Lee, Y. N. (2016). From age and gender to identity in technology-mediated language learning. In F. Farr & L. Murray (Eds), *The Routledge handbook of language learning and technology* (pp. 160-172). Routledge.

Geertz, C. (1973). *The interpretation of cultures: selected essays.* Basic Books.

Gitlin, T. (1980). *The whole world is watching: mass media in the making and unmaking of the new left.* University of California Press.

Goffman, E. (1963). *Behavior in public places: notes on the organization of gatherings.* Free Press.

Goffman, E. (1974). *Frame analysis.* Northeastern University Press.

Goffman, E. (1981). *Forms of talk.* University of Pennsylvania Press.

Gonzales, A., & Hancock, J. T. (2008). Identity shift in computer-mediated environments. *Media Psychology, 11*(2), 167-185. https://doi.org/10.1080/15213260802023433

Goodwin, C. (1995). Co-constructing meaning in conversations with an aphasic man. *Research on Language and Social Interaction, 28*(3), 233-60. https://doi.org/10.1207/s15327973rlsi2803_4

Goodwin, M. H. (1990). *He-said-she-said: talk as social organization among black children.* Indiana University Press.

References

Gorski, P. C. (2008). Good intentions are not enough: a decolonizing intercultural education. *Intercultural Education, 19*(6), 515-525. https://doi.org/10.1080/14675980802568319

Greenwood, J. (2005). Conflict resolution and mediation techniques. In M. Arnold, L. Heyne & J. Busser (Eds), *Problem solving: tools and techniques for the park and recreation administrator* (4th edition, pp. 111-127). Sagamore Publishing.

Guichon, N., & Cohen, C. (2016). Multimodality and CALL. In F. Farr & L. Murray (Eds), *The Routledge handbook of language learning and technology* (pp. 509-521). Routledge.

Guichon, N., & Wigham, C. R. (2016). A semiotic perspective on webconferencing supported language teaching. *ReCALL, 28*(1), 62-82. https://doi.org/10.1017/S0958344015000178

Gumperz, J. (1982). *Language and social identity*. Cambridge University Press.

Guth, S., & Helm, F. (2010). Introduction. In S. Guth & F. Helm (Eds), *Telecollaboration 2.0: language, literacy and intercultural learning in the 21st century* (pp. 13-35). Peter Lang. https://doi.org/10.3726/978-3-0351-0013-6

Hall, J. K., & Walsh, M. (2002). Teacher-student interaction and language learning. *Annual Review of Applied Linguistics, 22*, 186-203. https://doi.org/10.1017/S0267190502000107

Hamilton, H. E. (1994). *Conversations with an Alzheimer's patient*. Cambridge University Press. https://doi.org/10.1017/CBO9780511627774

Hampel, R., & Hauck, M. (2006). Computer-mediated language learning: making meaning in multimodal virtual learning spaces. *JALT-CALL Journal, 2*(2), 3-18.

Hampel, R., & Stickler, U. (2012). The use of videoconferencing to support multimodal interaction in an online language classroom. *ReCALL, 24*(2), 116-137. https://doi.org/10.1017/S095834401200002X

Hanna, B. E., & de Nooy, J. (2003). A funny thing happened on the way to the forum: electronic discussion and foreign language learning. *Language Learning & Technology, 7*(1), 71-85. http://llt.msu.edu/vol7num1/pdf/hanna.pdf

Hanna, B. E., & de Nooy, J. (2009). *Learning language and culture via public Internet discussion forums*. Palgrave Macmillan. https://doi.org/10.1057/9780230235823

Harrison, R., & Thomas, M. (2009). Identity in online communities: social networking sites and language learning. *International Journal of Emerging Technologies and Society, 7*(2), 109-124.

Hauck, M., Galley, R., & Warnecke, S. (2016). Researching participatory literacy and positioning in online learning communities. In F. Farr & L. Murray (Eds), *The Routledge handbook of language learning and technology* (pp. 71-87). Routledge.

Helm, F. (2013). A dialogic model for telecollaboration. *Bellaterra Journal of Teaching & Learning Language & Literature, 6*(2), 28-48. http://revistes.uab.cat/jtl3/article/view/522/571

Helm, F. (2014). Developing digital literacies through virtual exchange. *Elearning Papers, 38.* http://www.openeducationeuropa.eu/en/article/Developing-digital-literacies-through-virtual-exchange

Helm, F. (2017). Critical approaches to online intercultural language education. In S. L. Thorne & S. May (Eds), *Language, education and technology. Encyclopedia of language and education* (3rd ed., pp. 219-231). Springer, Cham. https://doi.org/10.1007/978-3-319-02237-6_18

Helm, F., & Dooly, M. (2017). Challenges in transcribing multimodal data: a case study. *Language Learning & Technology, 21*(1), 166-185. https://dx.doi.org/10125/44600

Heritage, J. (1988). Explanation as accounts: a conversational analytic perspective. In C. Antaki (Ed.), *Analysing everyday explanations.* Sage.

Heritage, J. (2005). Conversational analysis and institutional talk. In K. L. S Fitch (Ed.), *Handbook of language and social interaction.* Lawrence Erlbaum Associates, Inc.

Heritage, J. (2012). Epistemics in action: action formation and territories of knowledge. *Research on Language and Social Interaction, 45,* 1-25. https://doi.org/10.1080/08351813.2012.646684

Herring, S. C. (2007). A faceted classification scheme for computer-mediated discourse. *Language@Internet, 4.* http://www.languageatinternet.org/articles/2007/761

Higgins, C. (2009). *English as a local language: post-colonial identities and multilingual practices.* Multilingual Matters.

Hoey, B. A. (2014). *A simple introduction to the practice of ethnography and guide to ethnographic fieldnotes.* Marshall University Digital Scholar. http://works.bepress.com/brian_hoey/12

hooks, b. (1994). *Teaching to transgress.* Routledge.

Iskold, L. (2012). Imagined identities: an examination of self-authorship on Facebook. In P. Chamness Miller, M. Mantero & J. Watzke (Eds), *Readings in language studies: language and identity* (pp. 119-210). International Society for Language Studies, Inc.

Jaworski, A. (1993). *The power of silence: social and pragmatic perspectives.* Sage Publications. https://doi.org/10.4135/9781483325460

Jefferson, G. (1984). Transcription notation. In J. Atkinson & J. Heritage (Eds), *Structures of social interaction.* Cambridge University Press.

Jenkins, H., Purushotma, R., Weigel, M., Clinton, K., & Robison, A. J. (2009). *Confronting the challenges of participatory culture: media education for the 21st century. The John D. and Catherine T. MacArthur Foundation reports on digital media and learning*. MIT Press.

Jenkins, J. (2007). *English as a lingua franca: attitude and identity*. Oxford University Press.

Jenkins, J. (2014). *English as a lingua franca in the international university; the politics of academic English language policy*. Routledge.

Jones, A. (1999). The limits of cross-cultural dialogue: pedagogy, desire, and absolution in the classroom. *Educational Theory, 49*(3), 299-316. https://doi.org/10.1111/j.1741-5446.1999.00299.x

Kanno, Y. (2003). Imagined communities, school visions, and the education of bilingual students in Japan. *Journal of Language, Identity, and Education, 2*, 241-249. https://doi.org/10.1207/S15327701JLIE0204_1

Kehrwald, B. (2010). Being online: social presence as subjectivity in online learning. *London Review of Education, 8*(1), 39-50. https://doi.org/10.1080/14748460903557688

Kern, R. (2014). Technology as pharmakon: the promise and perils of the internet for foreign language education. *The Modern Language Journal, 98*(1), 340-357. https://doi.org/10.1111/j.1540-4781.2014.12065.x

Kern, R. (2015). *Language, literacy and technology*. Cambridge University Press. https://doi.org/10.1017/CBO9781139567701

Kern, R., Ware, P., & Warschauer. M. (2004). Crossing frontiers: new directions in online pedagogy and research. *Annual Review of Applied Linguistics 24*, 243-260. https://doi.org/10.1017/S0267190504000091

Klimanova, L. (2013). Second language identity building through participation in internet-mediated environments: a critical perspective. PhD Dissertation. Iowa Research Online. http://ir.uiowa.edu/etd/5001/

Klimanova, L., & Dembovskaya, S. (2013). L2 identity, discourse, and social networking in Russian. *Language Learning & Technology, 17*(1), 69-88.

Kötter, M. (2003). Negotiation of meaning and codeswitching in online tandems. *Language Learning & Technology, 7*(2), 145-172.

Kramsch, C. (2001). Intercultural communication. In R. Carter & D. Nunan (Eds), *The Cambridge guide to teaching English to speakers of other languages* (pp. 201-206). Cambridge University Press. https://doi.org/10.1017/CBO9780511667206.030

Kramsch, C. (2009). *The multilingual subject*. Oxford University Press.

Kramsch, C. (2013). Afterword. In B. Norton (Ed.), *Identity and language learning: gender, ethnicity and educational change* (pp. 192-199). Pearson Education/Longman. https://doi.org/10.21832/9781783090563-010

Kramsch, C. (2014). Teaching foreign languages in an era of globalization. Introduction. *The Modern Language Journal, 98*(1), 296-311. https://doi.org/10.1111/j.1540-4781.2014.12057.x

Kramsch, C., & Thorne, S. (2002). Foreign language learning as global communicative practice. In D. Block & D. Cameron (Eds), *Globalization and language teaching* (pp. 83-100). Routledge.

Kreber, C. (2004). An analysis of two models of reflection and their implications for educational development. *International Journal for Academic Development, 9*, 29-49. https://doi.org/10.1080/1360144042000296044

Kress, G., & van Leeuwen, T. (1996). *Reading images – the grammar of visual design.* Routledge.

Lam, W. S. E. (2000). L2 literacy and the design of the self: a case study of a teenager writing on the internet. *TESOL Quarterly, 34*(3), 457-482. https://doi.org/10.2307/3587739

Lam, W. S. E. (2006). Re-envisioning language, literacy and the immigrant subject in new mediascapes. *Pedagogies: An International Journal, 1*(3), 171-195. https://doi.org/10.1207/s15544818ped0103_2

Lam, W. S. E. (2014). Literacy and capital in immigrant youths' online networks across countries, learning, media and technology. https://doi.org/10.1080/17439884.2014.942665

Lamy, M.-N. (2012). Personal learning environments: concept or technology? Click if you want to speak: reframing CA for research into multimodal conversations in online learning. *International Journal of Virtual and Personal Learning Environments, 3*(1), 1-18. https://doi.org/10.4018/jvple.2012010101

Lamy, M.-N., & Goodfellow, R. (2010). Telecollaboration and learning 2.0. In S. Guth & F. Helm (Eds), *Telecollaboration 2.0: languages, literacies and intercultural learning in the 21st century* (pp. 107-138). Peter Lang.

Lave, J., & Wenger, E. (1991). Situated learning: legitimate peripheral participation. Cambridge University Press. https://doi.org/10.1017/CBO9780511815355

Lederach, J. P. (1995). *Preparing for peace.* Syracuse University Press.

Lee, E., & Norton, B. (2009). The English language, multilingualism, and the politics of location. *International Journal of Bilingual Education and Bilingualism, 12*(3), 277-290. https://doi.org/10.1080/13670050802153285

Lee, L. (2006). A study of native and nonnative speakers' feedback and responses in Spanish-American networked collaborative interaction. In J. A. Belz & S. L. Thorne (Eds), *Internet-mediated intercultural foreign language education* (pp. 147-176). Thomson Heinle.

Lewis, T., Chanier, T., & Youngs, B. (2011). Special issue commentary: multilateral online exchanges for language and culture learning. *Language Learning & Technology, 15*(1), 3-9.

Lewis, T., & O'Dowd, R. (2016). Introduction to OIE and this volume. In R. O'Dowd & T. Lewis (Eds), *Online intercultural exchange: policy, pedagogy, Practice* (pp. 3-20). Routledge.

Li, H. (2001). Silences and silencing silences. In *Philosophy of education studies yearbook*. University of Illinois.

Liddicoat, A. J. (2011). Enacting participation: hybrid modalities in online video conversation. In C. Develotte, R. Kern & M.-N. Lamy (Eds), *Décrire la conversation en ligne: le face à face distanciel* [Describing online conversation: face-to-face at a distance] (pp. 51-69). ENS Editions.

Liddicoat, A., & Tudini E. (2013). Expert-novice orientations: native-speaker power and the didactic choice in online intercultural interaction. In F. Sharifian & M. Jamarani (Eds), *Language and intercultural communication in the new era* (pp. 181-197). Routledge.

Little, D. (2016). Learner autonomy and telecollaborative language learning. In S. Jager, M. Kurek & B. O'Rourke (Eds), *New directions in telecollaborative research and practice: selected papers from the second conference on telecollaboration in higher education* (pp. 45-55). Research-publishing.net. https://doi.org/10.14705/rpnet.2016.telecollab2016.489

Loizidou, D., & Mangenot, F. (2016). Interactional dimension of online asynchronous exchange in an asymmetric telecollaboration. In S. Jager, M. Kurek & B. O'Rourke (Eds), *New directions in telecollaborative research and practice: selected papers from the second conference on telecollaboration in higher education* (pp. 155-161). Research-publishing.net. https://doi.org/10.14705/rpnet.2016.telecollab2016.502

Lugones, M. C., & Spelman, E. V. (1983). Have we got a theory for you! Feminist theory, cultural imperialism and the demand for 'the woman's voice'. *Women's Studies International Forum, 6*(6), 573-581. https://doi.org/10.1016/0277-5395(83)90019-5

Malinowski, D., & Kramsch, C. (2014). The ambiguous world of heteroglossic computer-mediated language learning. In A. Blackledge & A. Creese (Eds), *Heteroglossia as practice and pedagogy* (pp. 155-178). Springer. https://doi.org/10.1007/978-94-007-7856-6_9

Markus, H., & Nurius, P. (1986). Possible selves. *American Psychologist, 41*(9), 954-969. https://doi.org/10.1037/0003-066X.41.9.954

Matar, D. (2011). *What it means to be Palestinian: stories of Palestinian peoplehood.* I.B. Tauris.

Maynard, D. W. (2006). Ethnography and conversation analysis: what is the context of an utterance? In S. Hesse-Biber & P. L. Leavy (Eds), *Emergent methods in social research* (pp. 55-94). Sage. https://doi.org/10.4135/9781412984034.n4

McBride, K. (2009). Social-networking sites in foreign language classes: opportunities for re-creation. In L. Lomicka & G. Lord (Eds), *The next generation: social networking and online collaboration in foreign language learning* (pp. 35-58). CALICO Monograph Series.

Menchu, R. (1984). *I, Rigoberta Menchu: an Indian woman in Guatemala.* Verso. https://doi.org/10.1080/03064228408533778

Messina Dahlberg, G., & Bagga-Gupta, S. (2014). Understanding local learning spaces; an empirical study of languaging and transmigrant positions in the virtual classroom. *Learning, Media and Technology, 39*(4), 468-487. https://doi.org/10.1080/17439884.2014.931868

Messina Dahlberg, G., & Bagga-Gupta, S. (2015). Learning on-the-go in institutional telecollaboration: anthropological perspectives on the boundaries of digital spaces. In E. Dixon & M. Thomas (Eds), *Researching language learner interaction online: from social media to MOOCs, CALICO monograph series volume 13* (pp. 259-281). CALICO.

Miller, G. (1994). Toward ethnographies of institutional discourse: proposal and suggestions. *Journal of Contemporary Ethnography, 23*, 280-306. https://doi.org/10.1177/089124194023003002

Mohd-Asraf, R. (2005). English and Islam: a clash of civilizations? *Journal of Language, Identity & Education, 4*(2), 103-118. https://doi.org/10.1207/s15327701jlie0402_3

Möllering, M., & Levy, M. (2012). Intercultural competence in computer-mediated communication: an analysis of research methods. In M. A. D. Owenby & R. O'Dowd (Eds), *Researching online foreign language interaction and exchange: theories, methods and challenges* (pp. 233-264). Peter Lang.

Norton, B. (Ed.). (1997). Language and identity. *TESOL Quarterly, 31*(3), 409-429. https://doi.org/10.2307/3587831

Norton, B. (2000/2013). *Identity and language learning: extending the conversation.* Multilingual Matters.

References

Norton, B., & Toohey, K. (2002). Identity and language learning. In R. B. Kaplan (Ed.), *The Oxford handbook of applied linguistics* (pp. 115-123). Oxford University Press.

Norton, B., & Toohey, K. (2011). Identity, language learning, and social change. *Language Teaching, 44*(4), 412-446. https://doi.org/10.1017/S0261444811000309

Norton, B., & Williams, C. J. (2012). Digital identities, student investments and eGranary as a placed resource. *Language and Education, 26*(4), 315-329. https://doi.org/10.1080/095 00782.2012.691514

Norton Peirce, B. (1995). Social identity, investment, and language learning. *TESOL Quarterly 29*(1), 9-31. https://doi.org/10.2307/3587803

Nurullah, A. S. (2006). Ijtihād and creative/critical thinking: a new look into Islamic creativity. *The Islamic Quarterly, 50*(2), 153-173.

Nussbaum, M. (1996). *For love of country: debating the limits of patriotism*. Beacon Press.

O'Dowd, R. (2003). Understanding the "other side": intercultural learning in a Spanish-English e-mail exchange. *Language Learning & Technology, 7*(2), 118-144.

O'Dowd, R. (2006). *Telecollaboration and the development of intercultural communicative competence*. Langenscheidt.

O'Dowd, R. (Ed.). (2007). *Online intercultural exchange: an introduction for foreign language teachers*. Multilingual Matters.

O'Dowd, R., & Lewis, T. (Eds). (2016). *Online intercultural exchange: policy, pedagogy, practice*. Routledge.

Ochs, E. (1992). Indexing gender. In A. Duranti & C. Goodwin (Eds), *Rethinking context: language as an interactive phenomenon* (pp. 335-358). Cambridge University Press.

Ochs, E. (1993). Constructing social identity: a language socialization perspective. *Research on Language and Social Interaction, 26*(3), 287-306. https://doi.org/10.1207/ s15327973rlsi2603_3

Ortega, L., & Zyzik, E. (2008). Online interactions and L2 learning: some ethical challenges for L2 researchers. In S. Magnan (Ed.), *Mediating discourse online* (pp. 331-355). John Benjamins. https://doi.org/10.1075/aals.3.19ort

Pasfield-Neofitou, S. (2011). Online domains of language use: second language learners' experiences of virtual community and foreignness. *Language Learning & Technology, 15*(2), 92-108.

Pavlenko, A. (2003). "Language of the enemy": foreign language education and national identity. *International Journal of Bilingual Education and Bilingualism, 6*(5), 313-331. https://doi.org/10.1080/13670050308667789

Pavlenko, A., & Blackledge, A. (Eds). (2004). *Negotiation of identities in multilingual contexts*. Multilingual Matters.

Pavlenko, A., & Norton, B. (2007). Imagined communities, identity, and English language learning. In J. Cummins & C. Davison (Eds), *Kluwer handbook of English language teaching* (pp. 669-680). Springer. https://doi.org/10.1007/978-0-387-46301-8_43

Pennycook, A. (2001). *Critical applied linguistics: a critical introduction*. Lawrence Erlbaum Associates, Inc.

Pennycook, A., & Coutand-Marin, S. (2003). Teaching English as a missionary language. *Discourse: Studies in the cultural politics of Education, 24*(3). https://doi.org/10.1080/0159630032000172524

Phillipson, R. (1992). *Linguistic Imperialism*. Oxford University Press.

Phillipson, R. (2000). English in the New World Order: variations on a theme of linguistic imperialism and 'World' English. In T. Ricento (Ed.), *Ideology, politics, and language policies: focus on English* (pp. 87-106). John Benjamins. https://doi.org/10.1075/impact.6.08phi

Phipps, A. (2014). 'They are bombing now': 'intercultural dialogue' in times of conflict. *Language and Intercultural Communication, 14*(1), 108-124. https://doi.org/10.1080/14708477.2013.866127

Piller, I. (2012). Intercultural communication: an overview. In C. B. Paulston, S.-F. Kiesling & E. S. Rangel (Eds), *The handbook of intercultural discourse and communication* (pp. 2-18). Wiley-Blackwell Publishing. https://doi.org/10.1002/9781118247273.ch1

Piller, I. (2017). *Intercultural communication: a critical introduction*. Edinburgh University Press.

Piller, I., & Cho, J. (2013). Neoliberalism as language policy. *Language in Society 42*(1), 23-44. https://doi.org/10.1017/S0047404512000887

Rampton, M. B. H. (1990). Displacing the 'native speaker': expertise, affiliation and inheritance. *ELT Journal 44*(2), 97-101. https://doi.org/10.1093/eltj/44.2.97

Reinhardt, J., & Chen, H. (2013). An ecological analysis of social networking site-mediated identity development. In M.-N. Lamy & K. Zourou (Eds), *Social networking for language education* (pp. 11-30). Palgrave Macmillan. https://doi.org/10.1057/9781137023384_2

Richards, K. (2006). "Being the teacher": identity and classroom conversation. *Applied Linguistics, 27*(1), 51-77. https://doi.org/10.1093/applin/ami041

Riel, M. (1993). Global education through learning circles. In L. Harasim (Ed.), *Global networks* (pp. 221-236). MIT Press.

References

Rose, M. (2009). *21st century skills: education's new cliché*. Truthdig. http://www.truthdig.com/report/item/21st_century_skills_educations_new_cliche_20091208

Sacks, H. (1992). *Lectures on conversation* (volumes I and II, edited by G. Jefferson with Introduction by E.A. Schegloff). Oxford: Blackwell.

Said, E. W. (2004). *Humanism and democratic criticism*. Columbia University Press.

Sànchez, G. B., & Manrique, G. G. (2018). What makes our schools unique? A telecollaborative experience from the perspective of two 'new-comers'. In M. Dooly & R. O'Dowd (Eds), *In this together: teachers' experiences with transnational, telecollaborative language learning projects* (pp. 145-181). Peter Lang.

Saunders, H. (1999). *A public peace process: sustained dialogue to transform racial and ethnic conflicts*. Martin's Press. https://doi.org/10.1057/9780312299392

Sauro, S. (2014). Lessons from the fandom: task models for technology-enhanced language learning. In M. González-Lloret & L. Ortega (Eds), *Technology-mediated TBLT: researching technology and tasks* (pp. 239-262). John Benjamins.

Sauro, S. (2017). Online fan practices and CALL. *Calico Journal, 34*(2), 131-146. https://doi.org/10.1558/cj.33077

Savignon, S. J., & Sysoyev, P. V. (2002). Sociocultural strategies for a dialogue of cultures. *The Modern Language Journal, 86*, 508-524. https://doi.org/10.1111/1540-4781.00158

Schneider, J., & von der Emde, S. (2006). Conflicts in cyberspace: from communication breakdown to intercultural dialogue in online collaborations. In J. A. Belz & S. L. Thorne (Eds), *Internet-mediated intercultural foreign language education* (pp. 178-206). Thomson Heinle.

Schreiber, B. R. (2015). "I am what I am": multilingual identity and digital translanguaging. *Language Learning & Technology, 19*(3), 69-87. http://llt.msu.edu/issues/october2015/schreiber.pdf

Seedhouse, P. (2009). The interactional architecture of the language classroom. *Bellaterra: Journal of Teaching & Learning Language & Literature, 1*(1), 1-13.

Selwyn, N., & Facer, K. (2013). Introduction: the need for a politics of education and technology. In N. Selwyn & K. Facer (Eds), *The politics of education and technology: conflicts, controversies and connections* (pp. 1-20). Palgrave Macmillan. https://doi.org/10.1057/9781137031983_1

Sharma, B. K. (2012). Beyond social networking: performing global Englishes in Facebook by college youth in Nepal. *Journal of Sociolinguistics, 16*(4), 483-509. https://doi.org/10.1111/j.1467-9841.2012.00544.x

Shotter, J., & Newson, J. (1982). An ecological approach to cognitive development: implicate orders, joint action and intentionality. In G. Butterworth & P. Light (Eds), *Social cognition: studies of the development of understanding* (pp. 32-52). University of Chicago Press.

Silverman, D. (1993). *Interpreting qualitative data: methods for analysing talk, text, and interaction.* Sage.

Sindoni, M. G. (2013). *Spoken and written discourses in online interactions, a multimodal approach.* Routledge.

Soliya (2010). *Connect program facilitation training guide.* Unpublished training manual.

Stokoe, E. (2012). Moving forward with membership categorization analysis: methods for systemic analysis. *Discourse Studies, 14*(3), 277-303. https://doi.org/10.1177/1461445612441534

Sundqvist, P., & Sylvén, L. K. (2014). Language-related computer use: focus on young L2 English learners in Sweden. *ReCALL, 26*(1), 3-20. https://doi.org/10.1017/S0958344013000232

Sykes, J. M., Oskoz, A., & Thorne, S. L. (2008). Web 2.0, synthetic immersive environments and mobile resources for language education. *CALICO Journal, 25,* 529-546.

Telles, J. (2009). Do we really need a webcam? The uses that foreign language students make out of webcam images during teletandem sessions. *Revista Letras & Letras, 25*(2), 65-79.

Telles, J. (2014). Teletandem and performativity. *Revista Brasileira de Linguística Aplicada, 15*(1), 1-30. https://doi.org/10.1590/1984-639820155536

Thorne, S. L. (2010). The 'intercultural turn' and language learning in the crucible of new media. In S. Guth & F. Helm (Eds), *Telecollaboration 2.0: language, literacies and intercultural learning in the 21st century* (pp. 139-164). Peter Lang.

Thorne, S. L. (2013). Language learning, ecological validity, and innovation under conditions of superdiversity. *Bellaterra Journal of Teaching & Learning Language & Literature, 6*(2), 1-27.

Thorne, S. L. (2016). Cultures-of-use and morphologies of communicative action. *Language Learning & Technology, 20*(2), 185-191. http://llt.msu.edu/issues/june2016/thorne.pdf

Thorne, S. L., & Black, R. W. (2011). Identity and interaction in internet-mediated contexts. In C. Higgins (Ed.), *Identity formation in globalizing contexts* (pp. 257-278). Mouton de Gruyter. https://doi.org/10.1515/9783110267280.257

Thorne, S. L., Black, R. W., & Sykes, J. M. (2009). Second language use, socialization, and learning in internet interest communities and online gaming. *The Modern Language Journal, 93,* 802-821. https://doi.org/10.1111/j.1540-4781.2009.00974.x

References

Thorne, S. L., Sauro, S., & Smith, B. (2015). Technologies, identities, and expressive activity. *Annual Review of Applied Linguistics, 35*, 215-233. https://doi.org/10.1017/S0267190514000257

Train, R. (2006). A critical look at technologies and ideologies in internet-mediated intercultural foreign language education. In J. A. Belz & S. L. Thorne (Eds), *Internet-mediated intercultural foreign language education* (pp. 247-284). Thomson Heinle.

Train, R. (2010). Postcolonial complexities in foreign language education and the humanities. In G. Levine & A. Phipps (Eds), *Critical and intercultural theory and language pedagogy* (pp. 141-160). Cengage Learning.

Ushioda, E. (2011). Language learning motivation, self and identity: current theoretical perspectives. *Computer Assisted Language Learning, 24*(3), 199-210. https://doi.org/10.1080/09588221.2010.538701

Van Dijk, T. (1985). *Handbook of discourse analysis* (4 vols). Academic Press.

Van Lier, L. (2000). From input to affordance: social-interactive learning from an ecological perspective. In J. P. Lantolf (Ed.), *Sociocultural theory and second language learning* (pp. 245-260). Oxford University Press.

Ware, P. D. (2005). "Missed" communication in online communication: tensions in a German-American telecollaboration. *Language Learning & Technology, 9*(2), 64-89.

Ware, P. D., & Kramsch, C. (2005). Toward an intercultural stance: teaching German and English through telecollaboration. *Modern Language Journal, 89*(2), 190-205. https://doi.org/10.1111/j.1540-4781.2005.00274.x

Warschauer, M. (Ed.). (1996). *Telecollaboration in foreign language learning*. University of Hawaii Second Language Teaching and Curriculum Center.

Warschauer, M. (1998). *Telecollaboration in foreign language education*. Proceedings of the Hawaii Symposium (Technical Report Series). University of Hawaii Press.

Warschauer, M. & Kern, R. (Eds). (2000). *Network-based language teaching: concepts and practice*. Cambridge University Press. https://doi.org/10.1017/CBO9781139524735

Weedon, C. (1987/1997). *Feminist practice and poststructuralist theory (2nd edition)*. Blackwell.

Wenger, E. (1998). *Communities of practice: learning, meaning, and identity*. Cambridge University Press. https://doi.org/10.1017/CBO9780511803932

White, D. S., & Le Cornu, A. (2011). Visitors and residents: a new typology for online engagement. *First Monday, 16*(9). https://doi.org/10.5210/fm.v16i9.3171

Williamson, B. (2013). Networked cosmopolitanism? Shaping learners by remaking the curriculum of the future. In N. Selwyn & K. Facer (Eds), *The politics of education and technology: conflicts, controversies and connections* (pp. 39-62). Palgrave Macmillan. https://doi.org/10.1057/9781137031983_3

Zimmerman, D. H. (1998). Discoursal identities and social identities. In C. Antaki & S. Widdicombe (Eds), *Identities in talk* (pp. 87-106). Sage.

www.ingramcontent.com/pod-product-compliance
Lightning Source LLC
Chambersburg PA
CBHW020704270326
41928CB00005B/256